The ZAPPA Family Album

PATRICE
"CANDY"
ZAPPA

MY BROTHER WAS A MOTHER: TAKE 4

CREDITS

"My Brother Was A Mother: Take 4" was completed on November 26, 2021.

All photos are from the collection of Patrice "Candy" Zappa unless otherwise noted.

Layout and design by Greg Russo.

Fourth edition - November 2021. Third edition - January 2017. Second edition - November 2011. First edition - April 2003.

Copyright © 2002, 2003, 2011, 2017, 2021 by Patrice "Candy" Zappa.

All rights reserved, including the right of reproduction in whole or in part in any form. Printed and manufactured in the United States of America.

Special thanks: Greg Russo, Larry Rogak, Nolan Porter, Bob Zappa, Carl Zappa, Mari Linville, Lou Allred, Daniel Damico (Running Bear), Robert Elkins, Melissa Wilson, Eric Peterson, Alessandra Izzo, Ann Zappa, Deborah Zappa Katz, Ian Marek, Julie Waterman, Perry Ostrin, Christopher Lane, Glenn Leonard, Jack Fecko, Brian Vincent, Kilissa Cissoko, Javier Marcote, and Bobby Marquis.

Crossfire Publications, 54 Chester Avenue, Stewart Manor, NY 11530.

email: crossfirepublications@gmail.com

Check out Patrice Zappa's page on Facebook!

ISBN-13: 978-0-9983550-5-4

TABLE OF CONTENTS

Dedication (by Patrice "Candy" Zappa)	5
Preface #1 (by Greg Russo)	6
Preface #2 (by Larry Rogak)	7
Author's Introduction	10
Rose Marie Colimore	12
Francis Vincent Zappa	23
Picking Up Roots and Moving to the West Coast	37
Life in Southern California and the Stuff I Remember Most	51
Who Are The Brain Police? Or Random Memories of Frank	55
Life Marches On	58
Not "The Idle Meanderings of a Chemically Altered Imagination"	64
Frank Zappa "Abstract Self-Portrait"	65
More Trivial Poop or Life After Frank / Most Recently…	66
The Patrice and Nolan Section!	86
Recollections of Frank Zappa	88
Related Books and Music	115

(left to right) Aunt Fifi, Uncle Jimmy, Rose Marie, Francis, and Aunt Mary.

DEDICATION

I would like to dedicate this book to: my mother Rose Marie Zappa, father Francis Vincent Zappa – for their parental guidance, encouragement, protection and love; my brothers, Frank Zappa – for his brotherly love or in his case "Motherly Love," musical prowess and passing some of it on to me, and his amazing-ness and presence, Carl Zappa – for being my playmate and friend, and Bob Zappa – for being there for us all in times of need; my son David, and daughters Julie and Eva – for their love and support for my dreams and visions; my grandson Damian – who is more like his dad than he realizes; my granddaughter Eleanor – my little baby girl; and my late husband Nolan – my partner, my friend, my big daddy! It is also for my late friend, Vicki Mahoney – who remarked, after reading my book: "This book should be required reading for the L.A. Unified School District! Kids don't want to learn about the Civil War. They want to learn about Frank Zappa, dammit!"; Shirley Fisher – my longtime friend, who always rallied support for me in anything I did; Lou Allred – one of the biggest fans of Frank's that I know; Mari Linville – the lovely lady who introduced Nolan and me and is a great photographer; and Greg Russo, the other visionary who has written one of the best books on Frank, "Cosmik Debris." Thanks for giving my book a boost and beautifying it! And quite recently, Larry Rogak, my friend and lawyer who became one of my best friends and who helped with the launching of the last two editions. There are so many to list and you know who you are. I will always be grateful for your love and support and I hope you enjoy the new and improved edition of my book once again!

P.Z.P.

Yes, it's me with the best mother in the world!

PREFACE #1

Greetings, Readers!

I first met Candy Zappa at an Ed Palermo Big Band show at The Bottom Line in New York on August 23, 2001. Bob Zappa was there as well. Candy and I hit it off immediately. Not only is Candy a great vocal talent and performer, she has that unmistakable Zappa sense of humor. At the risk of sounding like Don Kirshner, I have recorded with her, and her ability to nail down a vocal in a short amount of time is amazing. All I have to do is sign her to my label so that she can have hit after hit! In all sincerity, it is an honor to know her and to experience her many abilities.

As for "dis here book," as they say in Brooklyn, this is the missing piece of the puzzle that you find years later in the back of the closet under all the mothballs, mouse droppings and other stuff that sticks to the floor. Who the fuck wants to clean it? Well, Candy has, and what a revelation! At last, here's Candy's first-hand account of what it was like living in the Zappa household with two devoted parents, two relatively normal brothers and her other brother Frank, who liked to act weird and blow up stuff! There's lots of stuff here I didn't know, and why should I because I wasn't there!

With this book, you are there. And we thought we knew everything about Frank Zappa. Ha!

This is a very compelling book by another Zappa that really knows how to tell an interesting and informative story. Candy, you've done a fine job that deserves a great deal of recognition. All my love to you and your family. I'm sure you'll sell plenty of copies before the record company pricks come to skim the cream!

As for everyone else, what the hell are you waiting for? Read on!

Greg Russo
July 26, 2002
Author, "Cosmik Debris: The Collected History & Improvisations of Frank Zappa"

PREFACE #2

When I interviewed Frank Zappa in 1980, one of the questions I asked him was, "Why do you have such a bad reputation?" His answer was, "Because everything you read about me is bullshit." And he was right.

My first awareness of Frank, if you can call it awareness, was through the ads that he ran in the comic books which I so avidly devoured as a child. Between the pages of Spider-Man and Fantastic Four, the following incomprehensible paid message would appear:

At the tender age of 10, I studied this ad, and his others, over and over, and could not for the life of me figure it out. Nothing in my working class Brooklyn Jewish home life gave me the foundation to absorb what this might be about, but somewhere within me was the sense that I had discovered an entry portal to some underground pool of knowledge that I would later come to know as cool stuff. (In 1967, "cool" was not a concept that had filtered into middle-class life yet.)

In 1973, at age 16, a high school friend brought over a copy of "Over-Nite Sensation," and upon first listening I had that sense that I had found something — perhaps the way an archaeologist feels when he brushes away some dirt and finds the top of a dinosaur vertebra. I played that vinyl album and meditated on it obsessively — both musically and lyrically. "I don't need your sweet devotion, I don't want your cheap emotion, whip me up some dragon lotion for your dirty love..."!! As a young man who was constantly getting in trouble for expressing myself in a clever and off-color manner and who never seemed to fit in with any crowd, I felt that I had found my messenger.

In fact, years later when I interviewed Frank, one of the memorable things he said to me was, "I provide reinforcement for people who are different." Perhaps no better summary could be made of Frank's life and works.

As I delved deeper into Frank's musical portfolio, I bought every album he had produced, discovered a network of fans around the country who had recorded his concerts on portable cassette decks and taped his interviews on the radio, and eagerly anticipated each new release. Just as important to me as Frank's music was his interpretation of the world. He cut through the window dressing and euphemisms that people use to avoid blunt reality and provided me with a road map to politics and sociology for those who are not willing to simply move with the herd, nor willing to just anesthetize their minds.

It became apparent from listening to his live interviews that there was a disconnect between what Frank said and what the press wrote about him. I yearned to know why he was constantly portrayed as such a wild man, a kook, a man who, according to legend, held a "gross-out contest" where he "ate shit on stage;" who "stomped on baby chicks," whose father was Mr. Green Jeans from the "Captain Kangaroo" show.

Meeting Frank became a goal for me the way climbing Mount Everest is a goal for some people. But how does one go about meeting a rock star? And why would a rock star want to meet me? Every celebrity has his or her legions of drooling fans, most of whom would give an arm to just touch them. But this was not idol worship. I wanted to talk with him at length about his ideas because he alone explained things in a way that made sense to me. And because ideas seemed to be so central to what Frank Zappa was, I had a gut feeling that somehow, he might someday be willing to grant me an audience.

I had already had a close brush with Frank. At a concert he gave at the State University of New York at Stony Brook in October 1978, I had managed to get front row center seats, and Frank had passed the mic to me to sing part of "St. Alfonzo's Pancake Breakfast."

Inspiration hit me in one of those rare moments in life that is truly cinematic. In 1980, while I was a second-year law student, one of my professors in a class on corporations was explaining how corrupt corporate officers manage to steal so much and get away with it because of certain immunities which the law confers upon them. He suddenly said, "There's a musician named Frank Zappa who once said, 'If you want to stop crime in America, put a cop on every board of directors.'"

At the time, Frank was involved in a long lawsuit with Warner Brothers over their release of the "Läther" album as four separate LPs for which they paid him no royalties. Frank had said much about this, in print and live interviews, and had even thwarted WB by taking "Läther" to a California radio station and playing the entire work on the air with specific instructions to listeners to tape it so that they would not have to buy the WB releases.

The proverbial light bulb turned on over my head, and the idea struck me: contact Frank's publicist and request an interview for my law school newspaper regarding the Warner Brothers lawsuit.

Conveniently, on the rear cover of the "Sheik Yerbouti" LP, was printed the name and address of Frank's publicist: The Wartoke Concern, located in Manhattan. I wrote them a letter, dutifully typed out on an IBM Selectric typewriter, the one with the interchangeable balls for each font (how quaint that sounds today!). In 1980, for the benefit of you youngsters, there was no Internet yet, no email, and word processing was just making its way into the business world. My letter requested an interview about Frank's lawsuit on behalf of my law school newspaper (for which I was, in fact, a reporter).

A couple of weeks later, I got a call from Jane Friedman at Wartoke. Frank was open to the idea. Some negotiations ensued, mostly centered around the fact that Frank's attorneys were concerned about his making public comments about a pending lawsuit. To seal the deal, I made a proposition: Frank and his lawyers could edit the transcript before it went into print. That clinched it.

It is hard to describe the feeling I had about achieving this goal. I was excited but not nervous. I had never conducted a formal interview, but I had so many questions that I had wanted to ask Frank for years that I needed no script. I was given instructions to meet Frank at a suite in the St. Regis Hotel in Manhattan on May 8, 1980. With me was a portable stereo cassette deck -- a rare item at the time -- and a camera.

My knock at the door to the hotel suite was answered by John Smothers. I had seen John at many a Zappa concert. If a bodyguard is meant to be intimidating, John fit the bill perfectly. He checked me out as though I might be a potentially dangerous person. After a few moments I guess he could tell I was harmless and I was led into a parlor room where Frank greeted me.

Show business people are notorious for being completely different in person than the persona they project in public.

Naive as it may sound, even for my 23 years at the time, I felt that Frank would be for real. And he was. He was friendly, gracious, and funny. We talked for three hours in the same relaxed informal manner as if we had done this many times.

Frank could tell right away that I was no journalist, but rather a fan who had found an angle to meet him. In fact, at the end of the interview, I confessed as much, to which he replied, "I know. That's why you're here."

After the interview was concluded, I transcribed the tape onto paper and mailed it to him. I next saw him backstage at the Palladium on East 14th Street on Halloween, 1980. He told me at that time that "this is the best interview I ever gave," and "I am making it part of my press package." From then on, whenever I went to one of his concerts and passed a note to him through a roadie, I got invited backstage.

Meeting Frank was my climb to the peak of Mount Everest. After that I felt that anything was possible if I put my mind to it. Best of all, Frank was everything I had hoped and expected. How much different an experience it would have been, what a crushing disillusionment, if he had turned out to be different in person than in public.

In 2008, I uploaded my interview with Frank onto the zappa.com website, where it was eventually seen by Candy. She and I have struck up an enduring friendship.

Today, I sorely miss Frank's voice of clarity about public events. I am sure he would be disgusted with the state of our political and social development -- even more so than he was in the 1970s and 1980s. He was truly original, musically and intellectually. But the time I spent with him has made an impression that is still strongly with me over 30 years later.

Larry Rogak
Fort Lauderdale, FL
September 18, 2011

AUTHOR'S INTRODUCTION

Being in the same house and growing up with Frank Zappa, was in itself, quite an amusement ride! Frank was eleven when I was born and in his own description of himself, he was five-foot-six with pimples and a moustache.

So how did this mature-for-his-age, cigarette-puffing teen that liked to blow up things for his amusement, progress to one of the most controversial, admired, respected and influential serious composers of the twentieth century?

It might have been hard for anyone to imagine a sensitive Frank Zappa that cared for his family, who protected, teased and played with his baby sister Candy and younger brother Carl and had a brotherly competition with his brother Bob; the Frank who butted heads with his father about which way his life should go; the Frank who, not meaning to, made his mother cry when he moved out of the house at nineteen; the Frank that welcomed his cousin Debbie, sister Ann, my friends, my ex-husbands and me backstage at his concerts.

I wouldn't have traded growing up with Frank for anything. I felt so grown up when I hung out with him. He wasn't judgmental or finger pointing and he had the best-bent sense of humor that became his trademark, enabling him to observe society's malcontents, foibles, diseases, and the occasional enema bandit.

Many times, when I was with friends, I would be introduced to them as "Frank Zappa's sister." Sometimes I wonder if they knew I had a first name! The list of questions went like this:

"Was Captain Kangaroo your dad?"

"Was Mr. Green Jeans your dad?"

"Is he your real blood brother?"

"Did he really eat shit on stage?"

"Is he as crazy as he looks?"

My favorite was, "Frank Zappa? I never heard of him."

Frank was a sane, brilliant man who took a lot of what he observed to heart, analyzing people and the things they did when it affected him. He wrote songs about what he saw, making it a musical book report, and he handed it back to society, to have a good look at itself, diseases, enemas and all.

I believe Frank was pretty particular about what he put in his mouth, so the "closest thing to eating shit (on stage or anywhere) was the buffet at a Holiday Inn in North Carolina."

Frank, observed as being weird and different growing up and as an adult, was nothing of the sort. He was a family man, however that term can be used, with a family that loved him, hooted at his antics and was devastated when he died. Chinese astrologically speaking, he was born in 1940, the year of the dragon, and like a dragon, he was a larger-than-life presence in this life. That presence most likely followed him into the great beyond. I'm sure when he got there, St. Peter must have greeted him with a fire retardant shield and a "Wow!"

Because I was still young and raised in an Italian-American family, my dad was old school and pretty strict with me, since I was the youngest girl. He was not happy about me hanging around with Frank. Dad felt I was too young to be exposed to the kind of things Frank was involved with, whatever they were in Dad's opinion. Then Frank married for the second time and went to raise his own family, and the responsibilities of a new family life and wife sort of got in the way. There was never any love lost between his wife and our family. My parents were nothing but cordial and gracious to her, sometimes a little afraid of her too, but that's another story.

There were lots more people in the real Zappa family, like grandparents, parents of course, aunts, uncles, cousins, two brothers and two sisters. It had to start somewhere! Frank left out a lot of stuff in his writings and that's all right. He was entitled to. I just hope that I have filled in some of the glaring blanks. No one's name was changed, guilty or not, and to know what life with Frank Zappa was really like, well, you'd have to have shared our lives and house with us. See, Frank wasn't just my brother, he was my hero: the knight in shining armor on the white horse or the benevolent dragon, waving his baton, conducting orchestras, composing some of the most astonishing pieces of music ever written in the world.

I am honored to have been chosen to be his little sister, to follow him in music. He told me once, when I was at his house recording a song I wrote, he said, "You sing well, Candy." I could take that to the bank.

The title for this book is ironically from Frank. In 1969, he was going to record an album of his songs with me singing and it was to be called "My Brother Is A Mother." With him being gone, I thought it appropriate to change the "Is" to a "Was" and voila! A book is born. Thank you, Frank. I love you and miss you.

Here I am at 4 with my dolly!

ROSE MARIE COLIMORE

Many decades ago, in a far-off land called Baltimore, Maryland, there was the Family Colimore. It consisted of my immigrant grandfather Charles (from Naples, Italy), grandmother Teresa (from Partinico, Sicily, Italy), and eleven brothers and sisters: Louis, James, Donald, Vincent, Florence, Mary, Fifi, Margaret, Rose, and Rose Marie. There was another one who died at birth. They were all born in Baltimore, Maryland.

Louis was only nineteen when he disappeared. It seems that he hung out with a rather unsavory crowd. One day, they were after him for some reason, and he was last seen knocking frantically at his sister Mary's door (no one was home to answer) before running off. No word as to his whereabouts was ever known.

Uncle Jimmy was, according to my mom, a ladies' man. He must have cut a dashing figure in his uniform, as he was a glider pilot in the US Army. In his later years, he sadly contracted leukemia and died.

Uncle Don worked for the Baltimore News-American newspaper. As most people did, he started out delivering the paper and worked his way into the office. In 1973, he was at my folks' house visiting for the first time in many years. He found out that he had stomach cancer and was given six months to live. He died three months later.

Uncle Vincent was a priest but left to join the Army, and while there, he studied and got his Ph.D. in languages to later become a professor at Loyola University. He eventually was an Alzheimer's victim and later died from its complications.

Aunt Florence was the oldest of the girls and had a very sad life. She was married to Augustine DeMayo, an abusive, violent man who gave everyone grief as he saw fit. In his later years, he was this harmless, bent over, toothless fellow. The years were not too good to him, not that he deserved it. Florence died of colon cancer - no surprise there. Stress will kill you.

Aunt Mary lived a fairly good life. She and my mom were the closest of all. They lived together in their parents' house and worked together at the French Tobacco Company. Later, Mary married Robert Cimino and lived in a great house in Baltimore. She would later introduce Frank to symphony musicians, letting him have a first look at orchestral politics. Mary lived to be 96.

Aunt Fifi Delores was the social butterfly of the '20s and '30s. She was attractive, not that Mary and Mom weren't, she just used a lot more makeup! In those days, being seen by the right people and in the right places was even more important than it is today. She knew the right people, right places and manners. Fifi introduced my mom to my dad, even though, according to Mom, Fifi was interested in my dad at first! That evening, Fifi told Mom that she would be introduced to a college graduate that evening at the Italian Consulate Tea. They met and the rest is history. Fifi and my mom saw each other for the last time in 2003, eight months before my mom passed. Fifi, however, went on to live to be 101 years. She was married to a wonderful man, my uncle Paul Guest. He was a diplomat, which afforded both of them the opportunity to live in very exotic places. Fifi painted several pictures of two of the places she lived, Africa and Europe. Paul died in 2002.

Margaret was only two when she got measles and died, as did her sister Rose.

Rose Marie was born June 7th, 1912. When we would talk about her childhood, she would get a dark look on her face

Grandma Teresa (left), her mother and sister in this more than century-old photo from the old country.

Tomboy Mommy

and say, "my childhood was horrible." Reliving parents' lives through their stories lets you understand why they are the way they are. She wasn't as close with her mom as we were. Mom used to say how her mother would never pick her up and hold her, and that must have hurt deeply as she would tell me this just before she died at 91. Sometimes mental scars don't heal — it's called baggage.

Mom's life started out on Market Place, by the harbor. Her parents owned a restaurant called "Little Charlie's" and they fed the stevedores and other locals. It was probably one of the original "soul food" places in the '20s, serving up things like fish, fritters, collard greens, hog's heads, brains and other delicacies. There was story that Frank told in his "The Real Frank Zappa Book" about some man that came into the restaurant and he was talking to Teresa. He touched her shoulder and she said, "Don't a-toucha me, I killa you!" She was holding a fork at the time, and in Frank's book, she stuck him in the head with a fork and he ran out screaming. Truthfully, no forks were stuck in anyone's head in the telling of this story.

Mom was recruited early in her life to help out with the restaurant. While her siblings were off having a life, Mom was working at seven or eight. Later on, Mom went to the Catholic parochial Seton High School. She loved the school and

Vince and Rose Marie in 1923.

the nuns were very good to her. Mom almost became a nun, but her mother cried and carried on how she wanted Mom to stay there and take care of her. The IGT — Italian Guilt Trip.

Rose Marie wasn't without escapades of her own. Picture it: 1934 (the year before she met Dad), Baltimore, the local ice skating pond. Lots of happy skaters blowing smoke from their mouths, as the temperature was quite nippy. Twenty-two-year-old, rosy-cheeked, raven-haired, green-eyed and quite beautiful Rose Marie Colimore was lacing up her skates while seated on a chair when her boyfriend, a handsome, dashing young man named John "Bunny" (Bunny?) Cooke skated over and sat down next to her. It seems he had some rather pressing news to share; he had to go back to Canada because his visa was expiring, and, oh, he just found out that fatherhood was looming in his future. It also seems his former girlfriend was the lucky mother-to-be. Rose Marie stood up, looking down with disgust, and spat out, "Well, you can just forget about it and don't come back!" John, taken aback by what he thought was a callous remark, uttered, "But Rose Marie, I still want to see you!" Rose

Rose Marie Colimore at age 14

Cheesecake Mommy!

Mom's brother Jimmy

Mom's missing brother Louis, in 1922.

Marie turned her head away. He was still trying to win points. "If it's a girl, I'll name her after you!" At this moment, anyone else would have made a soprano out of The Bun Man, but Mom, ever the lady, just skated away. Life was fairly simple for Mom — she lived with her parents, and she went to work, came home, fixed dinner, went to bed and got up the next day to do it all over again. She worked, as I said earlier, at the French Tobacco Company in 1933, making $17.50 per week, which was a hefty amount in those days. Her boss, a kindly man named Lucas Girardville, would travel and bring back jewelry and lots of other exotic trinkets and would give Mom first crack at them. Not being one to desire these things, she would pick out what she wanted and later give them to her sister Mary. I loved to hear about her life. It was sad and funny, but the best was yet to come.

Mom's brother Don, holding his daughter, with Teresa.

Florence and Teresa

Teresa Colimore in the 1930s.

Charles Colimore

Mary

FRANCIS VINCENT ZAPPA

Francis Vincent Zappa was born May 7th, 1905, in Partinico, Sicily. He was reported to have weighed in at an amazing 18 pounds at birth. There were three other siblings: two sisters (names unknown) and a younger brother, Cicero Joseph. His parents were Vincent and Rosa, and they came to America in 1908. They lived in a small apartment on York Road in Baltimore. Growing up quite poor, their main source of food was pasta. As a young boy of eight, to earn money, Dad worked in his father's barbershop. He would lather up the men's faces, and his little hands would be so sore after a day of that. Whatever his dad would pay him landed back in his father's pockets for alcohol.

Dad's family

Ann Zappa

Reaching his teens, Dad went to Polytechnic High School in Baltimore. He then told his dad he wanted to go to college. Dad was given a sum of $75, and with that plus his bridge-playing winnings, he financed his education. After moving to North Carolina and while in college, he met and married Nel Cheek and later had a daughter, Ann, my sister. Dad was a very bright, intelligent, talented and resourceful young man. He had a band in North Carolina that played around there and was also heard on local radio.

Eventually, Dad graduated from college in 1931 and went on to teach at Rose Hills, North Carolina. He found the problem of racial prejudice (being Italian) and religious prejudice (being Catholic) a hindrance to his success, so he moved back to Baltimore. His wife, Nel, not wanting to go, stayed behind. After they divorced, Dad found living in Baltimore more suited to his taste. The night that Dad was introduced to Mom in 1935 would change both of their lives forever. That first night, Dad invited Mom to a college bookstore that had a beer garden in the rear, where she, in her own words, had "her first and last beer." Then she sat in the back of the classroom where he taught a history class before they went to dinner.

Mom and Dad dated for four years. In those days, long courtships were quite all right. Eventually, Mom's family discovered Dad's divorce and daughter and the shit hit the fan. This was an outrage! You just didn't date a man with a past like that. They would sneak out on dates and I'm glad they stuck with it, for if they hadn't, none of the original Zappa kids would be here! One night, they were talking on the front porch when Teresa came out and invited them inside the house. Teresa didn't beat around the bush — she came right out and asked Dad if he wanted to marry Mom. He said yes, and then the conditions were laid out. They had to live in the house there with Teresa and Charles until, well until. They were married on June 11, 1939. Frank Jr. was born on December 21st, 1940, and both he and Mom almost didn't make it. Frank's birth was breach, with the umbilical cord wrapped around his neck. With patience,

Two photos of the handsome graduate, my dad, in 1931. He received his Bachelor's degree in education at the University of North Carolina at Chapel Hill.

prayer and I'm sure a few uttered oaths, he emerged into the world and the delivery room of Mercy Hospital.

Here are some things about Frank that no one has seen! At bottom left is Frank's baptismal certificate. Directly below is proof of his smallpox vaccination, and below that is his First Holy Communion certificate.

Baby Frank and Mom

Vince and Jimmy

Frank and Jimmy

Aunt Mary and Frank

Frankie giving Mom a kiss!

Frank and Grandma Colimore

My favorite photo of Frank.

Frank during his "terrible twos."

Frank with Spot or Rover (I can't remember!)

Not long after Frank's birth, Charles passed away after a lengthy illness. Teresa sold the house and everyone went on his or her own way. The little Zappa family moved into an apartment on Park Heights Street near Mom's sister Mary. Mary would come to the apartment and help Mom take care of "Frankie." She doted on the little man and was always buying him clothes and toys. Mary was a great lady and a wonderful aunt. The family was trying hard to stay afloat, and Dad being a resourceful man, worked as a barber to pay his college tuition. Dad finished college with a major in history, but he eventually taught mathematics.

Three years later, brother Robert or "Bobby" was born. The apartment became too small, making a six-month stay in Teresa's bigger house a necessary one. Not long after that, Dad took work in the Navy in Miami, Florida, taking the whole family with him. They had Navy housing for $75 per month. During this time, Mom developed an abscessed tooth and she wanted to go back to Baltimore to have it taken care of. Dad took the whole family on this outing, as he figured if Mom went alone, her mother would talk her in to staying there, alone. To assure that would not happen, they all went. My dad was a sharp cookie! They ended up staying in Maryland and moved to a cottage located on the Army Chemical Center on Pulaski Highway.

Frank training Bobby to hold up convenience stores, while aiming for a vital organ!

Dad's side of the family. Grandma Rosa Zappa with her grandchildren. Bob and Frank are on the right.

Bob and Frank

Brother Carl (at right) arrived in 1947, I came along March 28, 1951 and once again, sister Mary was there to help with the new young ones.

Life was good on the Army Chemical Base, with Dad working every day and Mom tending to the children's needs and wants. But Life has a habit of getting in the way; young Frank was the target of a bully who gave him a beating every day. Dad, sensing something was amiss with Frank, wanted to know what was going on and when Frank told him, Dad's response was for Frank to take care of that guy or Dad would take care of Frank. Dad never hit any of us, but his threat seemed to work: for the next day, Frank waited for the bully and wailed on him with the fury of a madman. Bobby was there and seeing his brother flip like that, ran home and told Mom that Frankie was beating the bully badly. Mom supposedly grabbed me

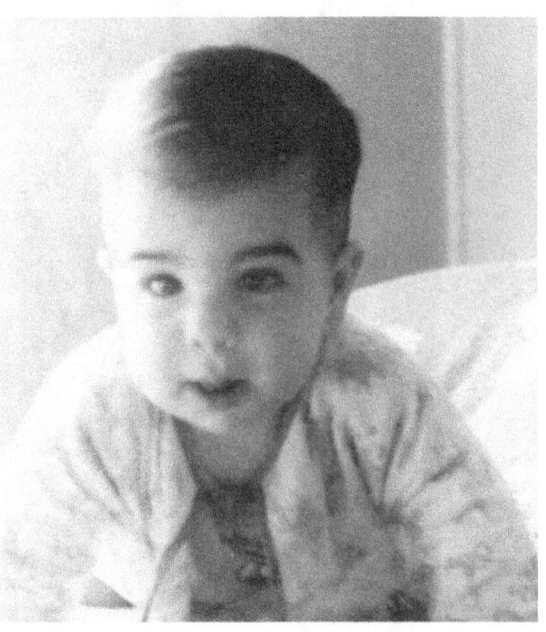

Bob

Above: me and Mom. Below: the notorious "Frankie Gang," with Frank and his unknown moll.

At right: Frank recruiting Carl, dubbed "Lookout," into the gang.

Look how cute I am!

Top right: me and Mom. In 1951, Carl nicknamed me "Candy" because he said I was so sweet.

Bottom right: Carl waits for me to get over a hangover.

and they headed back to the school where, by now, a large crowd had gathered, including the principal. Mom grabbed Frank and said, "Stop it, Frankie! You're killing him!" He stopped and they all headed for home, where Mom had a lovely pot roast waiting. It reminds me of the scene from "A Christmas Story" when Ralphie flipped at the kid that threw the snowball at him and he beat the snot out of that kid.

While the Zappa family was sitting at the table, enjoying their evening dinner, the phone rang and Dad answered it. It was the principal of Frank's school, reading Dad the riot act about the beating that "poor child" received from Frank, or as she put it, "Your son is a brute and a troublemaker, and what are you going to do about it?" If there was anything I learned from my father, that was to protect your children at all costs. He shot back, "What the hell were you doing when that poor kid was beating MY son?" The upshot was that Dad was to be at the principal's office the next day. He showed up, armed with verbal ammunition, and when the principal got a load of it, she literally ran out of her office and hid in the teacher's lounge.

The west coast had been calling to my Dad for some time, and when a chance came to teach metallurgy at the Naval Academy in California, he jumped at it. The letter arrived the same day the family came back from vacationing from Rehoboth Beach in Delaware. Dad was jubilant! Mom was not so happy, knowing that her life and that of the family, would be changed forever. The closeness of the Colimore sisters, Rose Marie and Mary, would be affected for the rest of their lives.

At right:
Mom and Dad shine like movie stars, with Frank, Bobby and Carl.

Eleven-year-old Frank (butt in hand), with Bob (8), and Carl (3).

PICKING UP ROOTS AND MOVING TO THE WEST COAST

There have been several books written about Frank and our family with the erroneous date of our moving to California as November 1950. We came to California in December 1951, the year I was born. It would be kind of hard to come out here in 1950, go back to Baltimore, Maryland for my mother to have me and come back the next year. We traveled in a car called a Henry J, and Frank described sitting in the back seat of the car like sitting on an ironing board. We moved to Monterey, California with all expenses paid by the US Navy. My dad was commissioned to teach metallurgy, and don't ask me what that is! Not long after we moved into the house, someone rang our doorbell. When Dad went to see who was there, the only thing on the porch was a large basket with baby things in it — diapers, food, toys, etc. They never found out who left it.

Monterey didn't offer much in the way of adolescent entertainment, so Frank made his own fun by blowing things up. Mom and Dad were aware of his love of the BOOM! That's why they refused to buy him a chemistry set, knowing what would happen. Frank went to the garage and loaded a toilet paper roll with some explosive stuff and lit it. Unfortunately, it was sitting near his family jewels, and when it went off, it blew him back a foot. He almost became a childless man.

In 1954, my brother Carl's health was in jeopardy and it was recommended that we move to a cooler and more moist climate. We moved to San Diego, and Frank, still enamored with blowing things up, performed one of his finest moments with the help of some friends. It was Open House night at his school, and these boys placed smoke bombs in all the lavatories. Getting caught was inevitable, and the next day, with Carl and me in tow, Mom and Frank went to the fire station. I was amused by Frank's demeanor but worried that he would get in trouble. Even at that young age, I admired anything Frank did, good or bad. A policewoman came in and took Carl and me outside to play with a puppy that someone had brought in. This way, Frank could be reprimanded without us seeing it. Mom was very upset and promised the fire marshal that she would see that Frank obeyed the rules.

The fifties: threats of nuclear bombs, fire drills, Howdy Doody, and door-to-door salesmen were common. Today they are called Jehovah's Witnesses. One day, a photographer salesman came to the door wanting to sell Mom the opportunity of him taking a picture of me. I had, at that time, what was referred to as "white coat fear," being afraid of doctors — they wear white coats and give shots! I saw his white coat, thought he was a doctor and went into psychotic mode, screaming into my room, slamming the door. Mom came in, trying to convince me to come out, but I wouldn't budge. Bob tried his best, to no avail. Frank came in with a "no-nonsense" look on his face, telling me the man was there to take my picture, not give me a shot and to get my little butt out there. OK, now I'll go. Frank was like that; he could get me to do just about anything. You can see the picture of me sitting on the sofa, holding my dollie upside down with an "I'm not too sure about this" look on my face.

In 1956, another family departure saw us moving to Lancaster, California. Frank discovered the cultural life of the desert and the infamous Denny's coffee shop, girls, and then music. Being in Lancaster was, in Frank's words, "the worst time of my life," and hearing him and Dad argue about things might have had something to do with it. After Grandmother Teresa passed on, she left a little money to Mom, and she and Dad bought a house in Lancaster, a nice three-bedroom house with a yard and a detached garage.

Frank had a girlfriend, Sandy Van Kamp. I thought she was cute, but Dad didn't like her and he was quite visible in his

Dad, the meteorologist

Dad in a professorial pose and two pictures of a helicopter that he wanted to buy. He didn't get it!

disenchantment of her and Frank. Whenever she came over and they headed for Frank's room, I would try to follow them so I could play with them, but Dad would stop me and occupy me with other things, like reading to him out of one of his math books while he kept a fatherly watch on Frank's door.

One of my favorite things to do when I came home from school was to make a big glass of chocolate milk and watch "American Bandstand." I had the biggest crush on Dick Clark, which Frank teased me about. Sometimes Frank would play his rock and roll or R&B music and I would sit and listen with him and he would dance with me and spin me around. Soon, music would be the focus of his life.

Frank formed a band called The Blackouts, aptly named because the other guys would drink peppermint schnapps until they would, what? Blackout! It was comprised of Johnny Franklin, Peter Lovio, Wally Salazar, and a couple other guys for which I don't remember their names. Hell, I was only six. They would rehearse and Mom would pick Frank up and bring him home, but my dad got mad and told her not to be his taxi. To Dad, if Frank could get to rehearsal, then he could get home. There were many heated debates over that. Lancaster would be the place where Frank met and went to school with Don Vliet, later to become Captain Beefheart. Don had an Oldsmobile with a werewolf head on his steering wheel. They would cruise the streets of Lancaster looking for girls. I liked Don — he was nice to my family and me. Frank told me that he used to go to Don's and listen to records while Don and Frank would eat pastries and drink Pepsi, which Don would yell at his Mom, Sue, to bring.

Other things happened in Lancaster. I met my sister Ann and her kids for the first time when I was six. Frank went to the police and told them that Dad had kicked him out of the house. Frank graduated from high school in 1958. One fun time in particular (I hope the sarcasm is evident here), was the day our parents took Carl and me to the hospital to have our tonsils taken out! We were awakened early one morning, being told we were going on a trip. We went on a trip all right — to the hospital! Talk about white coat fear; I was in abject terror! You'd think I was getting murdered when they had to give me the shot to put me to sleep. To get even, I made Mom stay overnight on a cot. I wasn't the only one who had a fear of doctors. Frank was the same way. In fact, lots of children and adults are scared of doctors, but that's something

The official family portrait in formal attire.
(left to right: Dad, Frank, Bob [back], Carl [front], Mom [back], me [front])

you either get over or you don't. Fortunately, I did. The lack of fear comes in handy when making one's own doctor's appointments and keeping them.

Another time in good old Lancaster: one night, there was a knock at the door and Frank answered it. There were some white boys from school that were telling Frank that he had the "wrong people" in his band. A scuffle soon ensued. Bobby heard it and went out to help Frank. They sent the boys off with their tails between their legs, or in their cases, their heads up their asses. Talent didn't have color as far as Frank was concerned. I feel the same way.

After Frank graduated in 1958, we moved to Claremont to a house on Saint Augustine Street. This particular day, Dad had been on a fruit and veggie gathering errand from the local fruit and veggie stands there in Chino. On his way back, he noticed that oxygen was scarce. I think it's described as a gorilla sitting on your chest. He pulled over to the side of the road, and thinking he was about to breathe his last, he recovered long enough to drive home. Upon entering the house, Mom saw how pale and listless he was, made him lie down on the couch and called Dr. Illsley (how appropriate! — like Dr. Payne for a dentist). He instructed Mom to get him to the hospital. Dad smoked Chesterfield Kings and I would imagine that at the time, smoking was the last thing on his mind. Mom gave Frank instructions to take care of us kids while she drove Dad to the hospital. He stayed there for a while and recovered slowly.

Mom with all four kids at Knott's Berry Farm:
(top) Bob, Frank; (bottom) me, Carl.

Frank on the drums with his early band The Blackouts.

Frank had been planning to move out, but Mom insisted he stay long enough to help out until Dad recovered. The friction between Dad and Frank grew to a head, and at times, they hardly spoke to each other.

Their personalities seemed to be at diverse ends of each other. Dad was not a mushy, flowery kind of guy, but he showed his care for his family in tangible ways; food on the table, roof over our heads, fulfilling our needs in whatever way he could. Frank would, in his own way, demonstrate different ways, but still caring. Mom was our spiritual provider, making sure we went to church, cooking good and healthy meals and making sure we had clean clothes. You can never have enough clean underwear.

Being brought up Catholic, we went to parochial school, and in fact, eight out of my twelve years of school were spent genuflecting and making the sign of the cross. Frank and Bob were so bored in church, much to Mom's consternation, and I'm sure they wished they could be anywhere else.

During school hours, we were herded into the church on holy days and packed into the pews like sardines. It was usually warm with all the body heat, and invariably, some child who had fasted would get ill and puke. One day the girl next to me unloaded the contents of her stomach all over my shoes! I wanted so much to leave, but the nun told me to stay put. I was forced to stay with the girl's breakfast decorating my shoes. She, obviously, was not going to receive communion and neither was I.

This very rare photo of Frank with The Blackouts is not in the greatest shape, but it does show Frank's girlfriend, Sandy Van Kamp. Bob is next to Frank.

At right is me in front of our car. Some people think that they can see Frank in this photo!

My First Communion

Carl at his Confirmation, with Bob

The whole family (left to right): Frank, Bob, me, Mom, Dad, and Carl.

The tension between Frank and Dad was hard to live with, and even at my young age of eight, I didn't really have anyone to talk to about it. I did, however, confide in a fellow schoolmate about it, though. I think I told her, "I don't think my dad likes my brother." Dad wanted Frank to follow in his footsteps and be an engineer, but the type of engineer Frank wanted to be was the kind that drove his personal music train on the track to his destiny. Frank eventually moved out of the house when he was nineteen. That day, Mom cried inconsolably. There was nothing I could say to make her feel better, so I just sat with her and held her hand. There was still a line of communication between them though, and one day Frank called Mom telling her he was starving and if could he get some money. Mom made up a care package of toiletries, clothes, some food and $50 (a lot of money then), and sent it with Bobby, on the bus, to Frank. Frank survived and chose to go to Chaffey Junior College for the "express purpose of meeting girls." And a girl he met! It was his future wife, Kay Sherman. Kay was a willowy blonde with a soft voice and a pleasant personality. Before you could say "Great Googly Moogly," they had moved in together. They had a great house on "G" Street in Ontario, CA. It was an old house with an attic and a basement. Frank had put all of his artwork in the basement and I loved going there. It smelled old and musty, but it was a great place. I still get a certain feeling when I think about it: it was where Frank was.

Mom took Carl and me over to their house one night. Dad wouldn't go because he didn't think it was proper for a man and woman to live together without being married. He didn't want us to go either, but we went anyway. They had cats and candy, two of my favorite things! As soon as I found that out, I asked to see the cats and was shown the way. Lots of kitties to play with! Kay was a wonderful, if not a nervous hostess and offered Carl and me lemon drops. They soon became my favorite sweet. It was all a little tense but cordial, with Mom's careful eye watching everything. Frank and Kay also had a great record collection. Who remembers vinyl and record players (or stereo hi-fis as they were called)?

As I wandered around, I noticed Kay in the bathroom seated at her vanity (remember those?) fixing her hair. I walked in and noticed a large note on the mirror that read "Take Your Pill." I asked her what that meant. She explained that it was a pill so she wouldn't have kids. I said, "They have pills for that?" What will they think of next?

Frank and Kay married, but not before Mom signed for Frank, as he was only 20 and Kay was 21.

Nineteen sixty was a year of change for everyone - a new president, Camelot, my brother Bob went into the Marines, and with no work for my dad in California, he was offered a teaching job in Sarasota, Florida. We headed south, and what a culture shock that was for us. Being used to living the easy, smoggy, dry California life, now we were in humidity, daily thunderstorms in the summer and sharing a huge old house with other people. It was quite an eye opener. It was there that I sprouted boobs and started my period, at ten years of age. My father was beside himself! Like I planned it or something!

The existence there in the south wasn't like anything we'd ever known, but we made the best of it. Eventually we got homesick for California, and even though the school offered my dad housing, which he tried to talk us in to taking, and a permanent job to teach there, we opted to go home. We missed Frank, the kitties, the smog and California and headed out as soon as we could. We arranged to stay with Frank until we found a house. I remember the day we pulled into Frank's driveway and he came out with a big smile on his face yelling, "Hey!" I was so happy to see him. I ran to him and hugged him and said, "Where are the cats?" We all piled in and Kay was as gracious as she could be under

Two photos of Frank with his first wife, Kay Sherman.

the circumstances, showing us all where we were to sleep. I loved being there in that old house; I wished I could have lived there forever. Like I said, it was where Frank was and I wished I could have stayed with him forever too. He was my big brother and he could get me to do anything, and one day he did.

By then, my dad had found a three-bedroom, two-bath house with a yard and detached garage in Montclair, California and only paid one dollar to get in. Don't ask me how that happened, but I have the paperwork to prove it! We moved in and loved the house. It was a warm place that my parents kept quite nice, especially for entertaining their friends. One day, Frank, Kay and her parents came over for a visit, and Frank, being an instigator, pulled me in the kitchen and was looking for mischief to get into. He opened the freezer and saw a bowl of fava beans, which looked like little turds. His eyes lit up like a Christmas tree and he handed me the bowl and said, "Candy, go offer these to Kay's folks!" Well, I wasn't going to do anything of the sort but he insisted, offering me anything I wanted to just go do it. "Oh all right," I thought, what harm could it do? So, out into the living room I trotted, holding this bowl of yucky looking brown things, huddled sticky-like together. I held it out to Kay's mom and Dad and with all the hostess-with-the-mostess tone of voice I could muster, and I said, "Would you like one of these?" They looked at each other like I had lobsters crawling out of my ears and I caught a glimpse of my parents looking at each other nervously. With as much politeness mixed with inhibited revulsion, Kay's mother said, "Oh, no thank you, dear." I nodded and smiled and went back into the kitchen where Frank was on the floor rolling back and forth laughing so hard, holding his stomach! God, I was mad, so mad I yelled at Frank, "What are you laughing at?" He got up and hugged me and very soon after that, he took me to a movie with Kay (I'm surprised she spoke to me!) to see a Jerry Lewis movie, as he was one of my favorite comedians at the time.

Left: My Confirmation in Sarasota, Florida in 1961.

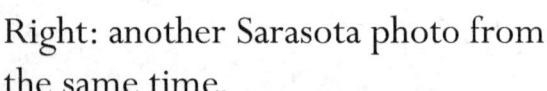

Right: another Sarasota photo from the same time.

All good things come to an end though, and one day Frank called Mom and asked her to come and get him, as he and Kay were divorcing. I felt bad for Frank but then I felt bad that there was no more old house with the artwork and kitties and lemon drops and records on the record player — the things a kid thinks of.

That didn't stop Frank from his life. He acquired enough money from writing the score for a movie called "Run Home, Slow" written by one of his teachers, Don Cerveris (starring Mercedes McCambridge, later the voice of the devil in "The Exorcist"), to take over his friend Paul Buff's studio on Archibald Avenue in Cucamonga. It later became known as the infamous Studio Z. I had heard about it and always wanted to visit there, and one day I got my wish. I was home sick with a cold and Frank came over in his 1963 mustard yellow Chevy station wagon (which, by the way, carried us cross-country to Florida in 1967) and he came in and asked what I was doing home. After explaining about my cold, he said he was taking me to see his studio. Mom was at work and I just knew she would not want me to go, but I called her anyway. I asked her if I could go with Frank to see his studio and, of course, she said no, that I shouldn't be out if I'm sick. I said OK, hung up the phone and turned to Frank. Hearing that Mom had told me not to go, he looked at me with this no nonsense look on his face (like he did when I wouldn't go get my picture taken when I was little) and said, "You're going!" I felt like he was rebelling against Mom with me as the bait! We got in his car and off we went.

I remember the smell of the place as we walked in; it so reminded me of his basement in the house on "G" Street with all of his artwork in it! He showed me the props he painted and built for his movie he was making called "Captain Beefheart vs. The Grunt People." Ironically, that's where Don (Van) Vliet got the name Captain Beefheart. It looked like a mad scientist's laboratory and a spaceship. Frank was like a kid showing me his work, so proud. I loved that he wanted my opinion, like it mattered. He had taken the cover from a speaker, kneeled down and put his head in it and talked, saying, "How does this sound, Candy?" As we walked through the studio, he asked me questions big brothers ask their little sisters like if I have any boyfriends. A frown came across his face when he heard my answer, which was, I wasn't allowed boyfriends. He probably felt the old feelings of being restricted by Dad when he was younger and it angered him. I did tell him I liked Jackie Gleason and that we watched his show all the time. "Jackie Gleason? He's just an old man with bad breath!" Yeah, like he knew. Soon, my time at Studio Z had come to an end and we made a mad dash to get me home before Dad got there. If he knew I had been out with Frank instead of being home sick, it could get ugly. I ran in the house and jumped in bed. By now, my fever had returned and I looked like hell, but I put on a good face when Dad opened my bedroom door and asked me how I was. Bravely smiling, I said, "I'm feeling better." For some reason, Dad blamed my mom when one of us kids got sick, like she was Florence Nightingale and it was her fault.

At this point, I was music curious, and finding my dad's old guitar, I started to play it. Little did I know that this would be the defining moment of my musical career. On Friday nights, Mom would make her famous chili and Frank would come over. This one Friday, he brought Don Van Vliet with him. I was in my bedroom playing guitar and trying to sing along with it. Frank showed me some major seventh chords to use and continued lessons for about a week, and as if I had graduated, he said, "You're on your own now, kid, get to work!" And get to work I did! I started writing songs like a crazy person, one after the other. It was like a floodgate opened up and all the creativity that seemed to flow through Zappa veins was let out! While I was in junior high, I formed an all-girl group and called it The New Dawn Singers. We performed for a few school functions, and Frank and his friend Lorraine Belcher were in the audience one night. He smiled big and I was beaming with pride. It was one of the best nights of my life. What a treat to have him there!

For some reason, which I couldn't quite figure out at the time, my dad told me I had to give up the group. I was incredulous, angry and resentful. Why did I have to give up something I loved and was good at? He wouldn't give me his logic for such a drastic action, but as I got older and after my Dad passed, I tried to figure it out. Frank was monumental in his career and my dad might have thought I was headed in the same direction. Not knowing he wouldn't live to see that happen, he might have wanted to stop it before it happened. He also was probably afraid that all the crazy things that Frank was doing would happen to me. Even though Dad wasn't there when I finally did achieve some modicum of celebrity with my music, I did have some crazy things happen, but thankfully I am still here, alive and kicking, to tell about it and write about it too!

"A Day At The Beach" — an early Frank Zappa artwork done for me.

LIFE IN SOUTHERN CALIFORNIA AND THE STUFF I REMEMBER MOST

Living in Southern California was great fun in the early sixties. The hippies hadn't really blossomed yet, but would in a few years. President Kennedy was making quite a mark for himself, and of course, Jacqueline was the talk of the world in fashion and beauty. Our lives on Palo Verde Avenue in Montclair were about as American as you could get. My mom was a total "Mom": up-to-date on fashion, housekeeping, cooking and being an all around lovely, warm lady. She was the best, and I'd like to think I got some of my Mom talents from her. Maybe we'd better ask my kids! She and Dad had a good marriage, although it wasn't without its snags, like the fights over Frank, which there were a lot of. Sometimes, I think my dad was a little jealous of Frank and how close he was with Mom. Men. Silly, aren't they? My dad was the epitome of creature comforts, and that meant coming home to a hot meal, watching television in his shorts and staying at home. Mom was an adventurer, so on Friday nights, our adventures consisted of her taking Carl and me out to dinner. In those days, it was customary for Catholics to eat fish on Friday, and I loved my shrimp dinners. I know shrimp aren't fish, but they aren't meat either. I was safe; I wasn't going to hell, at least not for that! After dinner, Mom would take us to the local TG&Y five-and-dime store and buy us a toy, and then to the drug store, where I would get the latest edition of Sixteen magazine and some candy. Then we went home to watch whatever was on television before going to bed. It sounds tame, but to us it was what we waited for all week. That was also the time Frank was on "The Steve Allen Show" playing a bicycle. That bike was mine! I got to stay up and watch him make music with my spokes!

In 1963, I was in junior high, Vernon Junior High that is, and I was springing into young womanhood. The only thing making it odd was that I had really hairy legs, I mean, dark curly, hairy legs. I would envy other girls with their smooth legs and wish mine could look like that. One day, I came home and told my mom I was sick of looking like a guy, and she, even fearing the wrath of my father, secretly took me into the bathroom and showed me how to shave my legs. Wow! What a trip! I was actually getting rid of the stuff of nightmares. I went to school the next day beaming with pride at my new smooth-as-a-baby's-butt legs and everyone noticed and made comment. However, I had forgotten to shave the back of my legs and there was a lovely strip of black curly hair up and down the back of my legs. Well, I went home and shaved completely. One Saturday, I was in shorts and some stubble had come out. My dad saw it and yelled to Mom, "Rose Marie, are you letting her shave her legs?" Sheepishly, Mom said yes and Dad hit the roof! He yelled that I was not to ever shave my legs again. That summer was the worst, as not only did I have to let it all grow back, it came back blacker and curlier than it was originally. Mom had gotten me into Pomona Catholic Girls High and they didn't allow knee-high socks, so I had to wear pantyhose. Ugh! Do you know what black curly hair looks like under pantyhose? One day in physical education, a classmate remarked how she felt sorry for me because I couldn't shave my legs. That did it. I went home and shaved from asshole to appetite and proudly wore my shorts. My dad saw my legs and looked at me like he was going to say something, and I just shot him a look that said, "Don't even start with me." Thus ended the leg-shaving episode.

One more story about PCGH. They had a dance that I wanted to go to, and my dad would not let me go alone, even though the nuns and priests were there to chaperone. He made my mom go with me. With Mom as my "date," we went and I had a decent time and met some guy named Tim who wanted to do more than dance. We went outside for a liplock, which wasn't that good, and I slipped him my phone number. What was I thinking? "Catholic Girls" was not written for me! Tim called the next day and my dad yelled at him, "She doesn't live here!" and hung up.

My sophomore year at PCGH, I was "commissioned" to learn about thirty songs (I was one of the few people who played guitar and had some musical ability to learn quickly) and teach them to my fellow classmates for a show that our speech teacher put together, called "…Around In Awareness," taken from part of a James Thurber quote. After school, for a couple of months, we rehearsed and were finally ready to put it on. Our first showing was for the school assembly on a Friday afternoon. It was a smashing success, well received, and it put me on the map! We did it again that Friday night and again the next night on Saturday. Back to school on Monday, we were informed that the show was held over to the next Saturday night. The cast was overjoyed at our success! Well, after the many nights of rehearsing in addition to the stress of school studies, I became ill. I was out of school the next day, which, I'm sure sent the director into a frenzy, causing him to send a friend of mine, who played classical guitar, to my house for me to teach her the thirty songs. She looked petrified as she stood in the doorway of my sickroom and I took pity on her. "Go home, Mary, I'll be there on Saturday." A look of great relief and joy came over her hand-covered face as she excused herself and, not wanting to catch whatever I had, ran out of the house! Mom drove me to the school and let me out while she went to sit in the audience. I had to wear a wig and black clothing. so the heat from the Kleig lights amplified the 103° fever I had. My throat felt like it was lined with broken glass and it took all my strength to sit upright on the stool while I played guitar and sang or croaked! During intermission, someone came to the dressing room and brought me an unwrapped peppermint ball, which tasted like heaven on my oh-so-sore throat. After the show, as I was receiving kudos for my performance, Mom helped me out to the car. I had thanked her for the peppermint ball and she denied having given it to me. She got really scared that someone gave me something laced with LSD, and I assured her it didn't have that as I am naturally on a buzz!

Other things that I remember about this time were helping my mom with housecleaning. We used to have a sit-down clothes presser and I loved to operate it. Mom also loved to rearrange furniture, and I believe I inherited that from her because both my dad and my ex-husband would say the same thing when they came home and saw that things changed; they said, "She's at it again!"

Dad and Mom made a good team, cooking team, figuring out the bank account team and parenting team. Dad would yell, Mom would make it all right. Dad was diabetic, another thing I inherited, and he loved food: bread, pie crust, pasta — all the things diabetics shouldn't eat. Things have changed, though. We can eat them only in moderation. Mom would make good dinners, lots of veggies and a main meat or fish entrée. On Sunday afternoons, she would fry chicken and have mashed potatoes, the real kind — not instant, veggies, corn on the cob and a salad. After dinner, Dad would take a long nap. He loved to shop for fruits and vegetables and he loved the not so common foods like smoked fish and pigs' feet. I was the only one who would sit down with him and eat them. Mom turned away, holding her nose. When it came to holiday feasts, they outdid themselves with turkey and all the trimmings. That was my favorite time, and the house would smell so good. I miss those days. I miss Christmas morning with all my family there, Frank and Bob checking out their gifts, and Carl and I opening up our packages and being thrilled. I miss the smell of early mornings in our house and everyone being there. I would love to pick a time and go back to it and stay for a while.

I remember going with my dad when he went shopping, and when we got to the checkout stand, he'd hold out some change and tell me to take what I wanted so I could buy a sweet. When I was four, we moved to San Diego, and every other Saturday after I took a nap, I'd have liver and onions with Dad and then we'd all get in the car and go see Roller Derby at the stadium. My folks really enjoyed that. It's funny what stuff you remember growing up. Dad loved us all and I think he had a hard time letting us grow up, maybe the way he wanted us to. Frank was a rebel, and on more than one occasion, Mom would say to me in exasperation, "You're just like your brother Frank!" I took that as a high compliment.

About 1963, my parents went into the restaurant business with Dad's brother Joe and it was in Upland, CA on Foothill Ave. It was called The Pit. Frank took the back of the place, built a stage and put up bamboo curtains, which the fire department promptly made him take down as they were a fire hazard. One night, he had Ray Collins and some other musicians there, and I asked if I could sing a couple of songs. Frank smiled big and told me to get up on stage and he asked Ray to sing with me. We sang "I'm Leaving It All Up To You" and I sang "Long Tall Texan." That was really the night the music bug got into my blood. The audience, which consisted of mainly college students, loved what I did and I had never heard that much applause! My parents were rather proud of me too. By that time too, at twelve, I was pretty well put together, like a brick house! Dad was quite concerned and really didn't want me to hang around Frank and his friends. It's a Dad thing.

Bob and his wife Marcia in 1966.

In 1966, Frank was working on his first album, "Freak Out!," and would come over to the house and show me songs he had written. I think I was supposed to sing one of them, but it didn't happen. After it was finished and released, he came over to our house in Montclair, wearing the fur coat he wore on the cover of the album, his hair flying in the wind (the neighbors took their children in the house when Frank showed up!) and he came in and put the album on our cheesy little record player. I thought it was awesome, since all I had been hearing was Beatles and Beach Boys. Then, "Who Are The Brain Police?" came on and Mom and I kind of looked at each other like we were hearing something otherworldly — "I think I'm gonna die, I think I'm gonna die.." Frank was so excited and he said, "Isn't this great?" I said, "It's bitchen, Frank!" I took that record to PCGH and played it for one of my teachers, and she just kind of stood there and stared at the record. I think she muttered, "That's really interesting." A euphemism for OMG! Another girl saw a picture of Frank in the newspaper; he was shirtless, sitting cross-legged on the bed, his black curly hair tussled, looking very handsome, and she came up to me and in a very snide tone said, "Is this your brother?" I said, "Yes, and?" She huffed off. What a loser.

By 1967, we left Montclair and went to Jacksonville, Florida. Again, what a culture shock. It felt like the people were like so far behind socially, but they academically surpassed anything California had to offer. I really had to work hard in school. At this same time, Frank had gone to New York for a while and it was nice having us all on the same coast. Being related to Frank had its ups and downs, and in Jacksonville, I would surely say it was the down part. It was like wild animals that see fire and yell and scream because they don't understand what it is. Almost every weekend, some of the local jock assholes would try to vandalize the house we lived in, and one time they almost spray painted the car, but my dad heard them and went out there before they could. Then there was the night Martin Luther King, Jr. was assassinated. Let me tell you what scary is. Being down south at that time was sketchy to say the least.

At the school I went to and Dad taught at, two students got into a fight. My dad tried to break it up and his arm was permanently damaged in the process. The school did nothing for him, so it was time to leave lovely Jacksonville. We were never so glad to get out of there. Frank was in the process of coming back to L.A., as we were, and he had wired some money for us to make the cross-country trek. We came back to Montclair in 1968, finding a place in lovely downtown Burbank, California and I graduated from Burbank High in 1969.

My high school graduation photo.

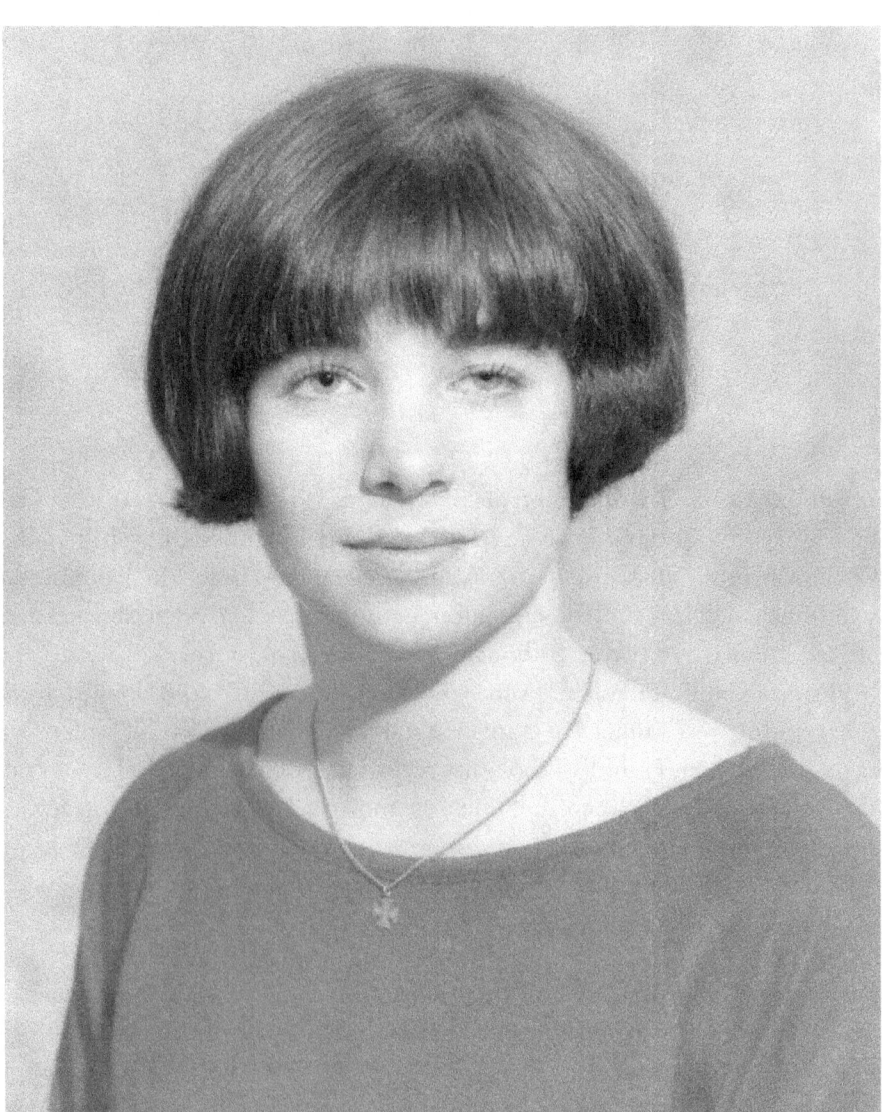

WHO ARE THE BRAIN POLICE?
OR RANDOM MEMORIES OF FRANK

As I mentioned, during the time that Frank was working on his songs for "Freak Out!," he would come over to our Montclair house and play the songs he had written and ask my opinion. I would say, "What's not to like?" I mean, let's face it, he was a brilliant genius, a monster guitarist and prolific writer/composer, and here I was this "bubblegummer" (another term for a teenie-bopper) who listened to The Beatles and appreciated other R&B artists (thanks to Frank and my indoctrination to the finer music of the time) and he wanted to know what I thought! Before he grew his infamous moustache, imperial and flowing long hair, he wore his hair in a greased back pompadour, popular at the time. One day, we went into the bathroom and I combed his hair down in the style of The Beatles. At first, he laughed at my efforts to make him look different, but seeing I didn't share his same view of humor, he looked again and thought, hmmm... maybe this might work. So began the transformation of the conservative pachuko-looking, Italian boy into Wild Man Frank, complete with the notable facial hair, which would soon become his trademark that he and the whole world would soon embrace. Sometimes he would stop by and take me out for a burger and a shake and we'd talk about stuff. Those were the most precious times, just he and I with no parental judgment, no intrusions. As our lives progressed, I'm sure there were times when he was concerned about me, but he had a full plate and he knew somehow I'd be OK. We both had destinies to fulfill. No matter how far away he was from me, we still loved each other and knew it.

In 1991, after I had found out about his cancer, I wrote him a three-page letter telling him how strong I thought his mind was and that he should visualize the cancer leaving his body. He had a tumor in his prostate that was so large, he was told it couldn't be operated on and he was catheterized for a year and a half. One day while I was at work, I got a call from Frank.

"Good afternoon, USA," I answered.
"I'd like to speak with Candy Zappa, please."

I could hardly contain my joy at hearing my brother's voice!

"Hi Frank, it's me!"
"Wow, you sound like a baritone in your old age!" he teased.

We talked about lots of things and he mentioned my letter. Then he asked me if I believed in all this religious stuff and told me that his tumor had shrunk and he wasn't catheterized anymore. I told him of course I believed.

"Well, I'm not going to poo-poo it anymore, I'll give you the credit!"

I told him I didn't do it and he should know who did. We ended our conversation with mutual "I love yous" and the rest of my day was so sweet.

One of Frank's favorite pastimes was making home movies, and since Carl and I were so obedient, he had two of the most malleable creatures at his disposal! He hooked up big lights in the hallway, dressed us both in black and had us dance our way down the hall as he filmed us. Then he'd stop the camera and take Carl in the bathroom. Carl had a pretty bad acne condition then and Frank thought it would be amusing to put a dollop of cold cream on the mirror and film Carl pretending that he was popping a zit. It would look like the zit exploded onto the mirror. I thought it was funny.

Something else about when we had the restaurant, The Pit…Frank was always experimenting with one thing or another, and this time it was pizza. He had this great idea to make a peanut butter and raisin pizza. In theory, it sounded feasible. On the plate, it was not so. It tasted like cardboard with dried-out peanut butter and raisins. If it seems like I'm jumping around in my memories of Frank, attribute it to my age, not that I'm old or feeble-minded, but I get to thinking about one time and another time pops up, so bear with me! Besides, I figure if you got bored by now, you wouldn't be reading, but if you aren't, hang on, there's more to come! These are, after all, random memories of Frank!

Case in point: 1965, Cucamonga, California — the garden spot of the San Bernardino Valley, on Archibald Avenue. Studio Z was Frank's haven away from the stressed-out life, where he could be the artist and musician he wanted to be and wasn't disturbing anyone. It seems word of his "Captain Beefheart" movie had made its way into the local newspaper and caught the eye of one Detective Willis of the San Ber'doo Police Department. He and his partner decided to pay Frank a visit, but not as detectives. They would disguise themselves, or at least Willis would, as his partner would hang outside listening to the banter on his wristwatch radio. Cheesy fuckers. Willis put on clothes that make him look like a used car salesman and he solicited Frank to make him a "sex movie." Frank, not wanting to cut himself short but knowing this guy couldn't afford a movie, told him that an audio tape would be cheaper, about $100. Willis gave Frank a list of the sex acts he wanted performed and the deal was made. Frank and Lorraine Belcher, his girlfriend at the time, made a tape of the noises and music they did and edited out the laughter. It was a "nice" tape.

Willis showed up a couple days later with backup. He walked in and handed Frank $50. Frank, not giving over the tape as that was not what he agreed to, told him the deal was for $100. At that moment, the police rushed in, confiscated the tape and other items in the studio and placed Frank and Lorraine under arrest. Of course, Mom and Dad bailed him out and Frank also talked them into helping bail out Lorraine too. Some of the money put together to release Frank came from Joyce, a friend of Paul Buff's wife Allison. As for the line in "Let's Make The Water Turn Black," "the neighbors on the right sat and watched them every night…," we were poison in our little neighborhood, and my friends weren't allowed to associate with me. It was stupid and sad. Things didn't stop there. Willis came to our house to try to arrest Frank again and my dad, all five-foot-six of him, wasn't afraid of that asshole, even though he was clearly a foot taller than Dad. He was on the front lawn poking his finger in his chest, demanding Willis get off his property.

After Frank achieved a good level of notoriety for his musical gifts, The Mothers played at some theatre on the Sunset Strip. We were invited to attend. Here were my folks, Carl and I dressed in our "go to church meeting" clothes and here were all these unwashed, leather clad, bell-wearing, feather-adorned hippies eyeballing us like, "WTF?" Oh, if they only knew who we were related to! When I was in Burbank High, I acquired a modicum of notoriety as "Frank Zappa's sister." I don't know if anyone there knew I had a first name. During roll call in my drama class, I was seated at the top of the auditorium by myself, nervously trying to keep my notes in order and make sure I had all my classes written down when the teacher announced my name, "Patrice Zappa." Without looking up and still scrambling for papers, I said, "Here." From the front row down below me, a boy turned around and yelled up at me, "Any relation to Frank?" Again, without looking up, I said, "Yeah, I'm his sister." And all of a sudden the whole class migrated up to where I was seated and I got very scared. They were asking me if I was really related to Frank. They were in awe and the teacher was having a fit, as it seemed she had lost control of her class. She ordered everyone back to their seats and continued with assignments. Another time, three boys were waiting at my desk in my English class wanting to know if I could get Frank to play at the school. I said I would ask. Frank said it would cost five thousand dollars and that was the bare bone minimum. So much for that idea!

I was fortunate enough to attend some of Frank's concerts, and one in 1969 was memorable. As Frank was performing at the Shrine Auditorium, some dimwit threw an orange and hit Frank in his privates. He brought the jerk onstage and instructed him to tear into the orange and eat it as he conducted the band in making "music to tear into an orange," and then told the guy to "get the fuck outta here!" At another concert, a bottle was thrown on stage and Frank stopped the show and wouldn't continue until the boob was found and escorted out of the place.

My visits to Frank's house were usually with Dad, and this one visit was really memorable. Frank was in his studio and he said, "Candy, come here. I want you to meet Jeff Beck." I shook his hand, saying I was glad to meet him, but I didn't know who he was. I wanted to scream when I found out a few years later who he was and that I shook his hand!

My favorite picture of me with my kids.

LIFE MARCHES ON

By the time the early seventies rolled around, I had been married twice with two children and I was no longer the "bubblegummer" but a responsible mom with kids, a husband and house to take care of. Frank had three children and both my oldest daughter and Frank's second son and our youngest girls would be born in the same year, a few months apart. That would be where the similarities would end. We were both parents but I was a full-time mom. Frank was a full-time musician/composer/writer, something I had always wanted to do, but diapers, chicken pox, PTA meetings and late night visits from Santa Claus kinda took up my time.

In December 1971, Frank was attacked on stage while performing in London, England and almost died. His thigh and several ribs were broken, and there was a hole in the back of his head. Frank came home with a full leg cast. One day, he came over to visit Mom, Dad and me. I saw Frank at the door and called out, "Hey Gimpy!" I don't think he liked that too much! I believe the line in "Dancin' Fool" was "one of my legs is shorter than the other and both of my feets too long" was written about this injury. Hey, go with what you know!

At one concert I went to with my dad (Mom didn't want to go so she babysat for me, what luck!), Frank sent a limo for us and it was great to arrive in it. Inside during the concert, I noticed a lovely pungent aroma wafting around and I believe that was my first contact high! I wonder what my dad was thinking as I swayed to the music, or was it the pot? Dad was proud of Frank, but I often wondered how he really felt — sad that Frank didn't follow in his footsteps, or just happy Frank made his way on his own terms, like my dad did. And maybe that's why they always butted heads.

In 1970, I was married and my son David was about nine months old. We lived in a small house in Burbank, and early one morning my mom came to my door and announced that Dad was in the hospital from insulin shock. Just two days before, they did a spread in Life Magazine about families of rock stars. Dad eventually came home and had gone from a robust, albeit overweight, 165 pounds to a frail 130 pounds. He would sit and watch television with a blanket on him, even though it would be eighty degrees outside. He came to visit me one day, and I just watched him holding my son David and was sad to see how frail he had become, his voice much weaker. A few months later, I had left my husband, David's father, and moved back in with my folks. On April 7, 1973, I had been invited to go to dinner with some friends. I was requested to be home by 11 PM. We went to Los Angeles to walk around and sightsee when I looked at my watch. It was 10:20. We rushed back, and I came in the house to find my dad's slacks in a pile on the floor, his shoes on their sides and Mom sitting watching television. My dad was a creature of habit. Every night, he would fold his pants and drape them over the chair at the dining

Dad in 1972.

room table with his shoes neatly put under them, all of his change on the table and any other items from his pockets. I knew something was wrong, and I went into the bedroom to see. My son was sleeping in his crib in their room, but I couldn't see Dad. I looked at the bathroom and the doors were open with the light off. I looked back at the bed again and noticed a short lump instead of a long one. I went out to Mom and asked why Dad was on the bed like that. She ran in and came right back out terrified and said, "Candy, he's dead!" I ran in and turned on the light, and sure enough, it looked like he sat on the bed and fell back, head turned to the side, eyes and mouth open, but with the most peaceful look on his face. He was afraid of dying (so afraid he wouldn't attend either of his parents' funerals), but mostly he didn't want to die in a hospital. Funny how wishes come true. After all the necessities were performed — calling the fire department, having Dad sent to the funeral home, calling Frank in Arizona — Frank canceled his concert and flew home. I told him how gray Dad was when I found him and he said, "Candy, I see musicians walking around all the time and their skin is gray." There must have been a need for a superb math teacher in heaven, and I believe that's where he is now. I had dreams of him for several years after he died. One of my favorites was of me on a train that stopped at a station; my dad climbed the stairs to get to the car I was in. He was wearing the blue suit he was buried in looking very handsome. I went to meet him, and he gave me a kiss on my cheek and I said, "Happy Father's Day!" Then he climbed back down and the train took off. Don't tell me we can't visit with our dear departed family members. I dream about Frank a lot.

In fact, three days before John Lennon was killed, I had a dream that Frank walked up to the front of an apartment building, someone called out his name and shot him five times, bang bang bang bang bang! I heard them as clear as if I was awake. The next day, I called Mom to see if she could find out if Frank was OK. She told me that he was sick with the flu and had to cancel his concert. Two days later, the same thing happened to John Lennon. I flipped when I saw the picture in the paper of the Dakota. It was the building I saw in my dream. My cousin Pat told me what happened was called dream transference, where I was picking up something that was going to happen but I had to put

Frank and Mom in 1973.

it on someone I knew. It happened to be Frank.

Three days later, at a concert at the Santa Monica Civic Auditorium, I went with my friend Shirley to see Frank. We went backstage, and after a minor altercation with his bodyguard Smothers, we got in to see him. Frank didn't look too happy. He was about to turn forty and his mortality must have been kind of evident, not that anyone would shoot him, but he was having health issues and didn't know what they were. During the concert, some guy was walking up the aisle with a cup full of condiments, mustard and relish. He was eating with his hand and somehow he got up to the stage and offered it up to Frank. Frank shook his head no, but the guy, not taking the rejection of his food offering too well, dumped it on the stage. Frank stopped the show and told Smothers to "take care of that guy." Smothers jumped offstage, grabbed the guy by the scruff of his shirt and the back of his pants and proceeded to rub his face back and forth in the sticky mess. Frank motioned the band to, once again, play some music befitting the situation, and then he stopped it. Smothers threw the guy off the stage. What a spectacle! The audience was driven into a "petulant frenzy!" That was one of the concerts that had a clothesline strewn across the stage with ladies undies on it, as someone was going to make him a quilt from those undies. There was a pair fastened to the bass drum so whenever it was hit, the panties would fly up. Frank announced to the ladies in the audience to send up their frilly, lacy panties and bras, and not the cotton, granny type. It was also the show with the infamous "voodoo butter underpants." I don't know what was in them, and I don't want to know. Frank asked me when were backstage if I had contributed my personals. I said, "No Frank, you don't want my orthopedic underwear!" He also made the remark that "Los Angeles needs a sense of humor…and a colonic" at this same concert.

Frank, nephew Jason and brother Bob in 1988 at The Beacon Theatre in New York City.

The years went by and I was lucky enough to attend many of Frank's concerts and they were always the best experiences. In 1989, I had gone over to Mom's for Mother's Day and she was sitting at the dining room table looking very sad. I asked her what was wrong.

"Frank called to wish me Happy Mother's Day and added, 'oh, by the way I have cancer'." I slowly inhaled like a painful reaction. We talked for a while and then I left and went to the church I was attending and asked the minister for special prayers for Frank. During the next three years, it looked like Frank's tumor was shrinking, but by 1992, the cancer metastasized and had gone to his blood and bones. During this time, Mom had gone to visit him and she told me that he was in visible pain and had a hard time sitting still. Then he sat next to her on the sofa and hugged her really hard, like he knew it would be the last time they would see each other. In May 1992, I had my last conversation with Frank. I asked him how he was doing and he said, "Well, Candy, I have my good days and I have my bad days. Today is one of my bad days." I told him not to worry, that heaven doesn't want him and hell is afraid he'll take over. He laughed weakly, but it was good to hear it. I also told him that I loved him and wanted to see him. He said, "Not now, we're on the same planet." Not for long, though. I had spent the night at a friend's house on December 3rd, 1993 and the next day, I called my mom to see how Frank was and she said, "Well, Frank's dead and they buried him already." I lost it, threw the phone down and sobbed into my hands. It was hard to fathom that his other family could be so callous as to not let us be there when he died, and then not let us know that there was a burial and to tell his own mother that he was buried already. Mom never got to see his grave, in fact, there is no head marker. Figure that one out. Life after Frank was sad indeed. Christmas became a non-holiday in my book. After Frank passed away, things weren't the same, and never will be. I felt so cheated out of not being able to see him, be there with him, and of course, none of our family was there when he died or was buried. I know our mother was very hurt at not being there, but she did see him one last time a few months before he died. Frank's kids never visited their grandmother, especially in her last few years when she was very ill. One day, after I had taken Mom for a wheelchair ride around the neighborhood, we came back and sat in her front yard. We were talking about Frank's kids and she talked about how they never visited her and then she said, "and don't you think that hurts?" Mom cared about Frank's kids, and it's too bad the feeling wasn't mutual. I told her that the important people in her life that loved her and cared for her were around her.

By 1994, finding a job in L.A. was impossible, sort of like now. I put my stuff in storage, told my mom that I was heading to Las Vegas and moved in with my friend Misha. I sat in with many different groups, but no one hired me. I didn't fit the prescribed formula at that time, I guess. I also met a good friend, Genaro "Jeep" Capone, the great grand nephew of Al Capone. His band played lots of good Top 40 and old-school stuff. His horn player, was the late Al Young, a wonderful, talented man. I ended up working for the Recycler and living in Vegas. It was good, but I developed asthma and bronchitis. Go figure — dry air and I got sick. Back to California and my daily dose of smog. I moved back to North Hollywood, on the same street as Mom. She and my brother Carl lived in the duplex Frank had bought for Mom and Dad. I moved back primarily to take care of Mom, who was at that time 82. I enjoyed helping her shop, setting her hair, taking her for wheelchair rides and staying with her, doling out her pills. I gave her a birthday party for her 90th, and it was videotaped. Now I have a wonderful, priceless memento of her. Mom was a strong little woman. She bore a great amount of sadness and held it in, which, I felt, led to a lot of her health problems. She had high blood pressure, severe arthritis in her hips and spine, and a barrage of other ailments that she didn't need to have. Mom took care of us all and Dad, and in the end, my brother Carl and I were her main caregivers. Mom was pretty strong up until she was 79. I loved to go to her house and make her lunch and sit with her while we pored over her clothes catalogs, and if I was lucky, she'd buy me something too. By 1996, I took over the driving duties, as Mom's sight wasn't that good and she drove too slowly. We would go grocery shopping, and that was a special time for her. It gave her a chance to pick out the food she wanted and it gave her some semblance of independence, even though I was right there with her. Those years from 1996-2004, before she passed away, were very good years. Every morning when I got up to go to work, I would stop by her house first and give her the medications she needed for the day, fix her some breakfast and then go. Carl took care of her during the day, and I would fix her dinner and put her to bed.

She didn't go out much because of her health, and in fact, had to forego her beloved Catholic Church services. A very nice lady named Mary brought Holy Communion to her every Sunday. Her faith was very important to her and it carried her through many of the tribulations she endured during her long life. As much as Mom was into her faith, that's how much she wanted all of her children to be. However, she sadly realized over the years that she was the only one who carried on with it. I had stopped going after my father died.

In 1999, I was introduced to Nolan Porter by our mutual friend Mari Linville at a restaurant. We got up to sing a song together and that was it. We sounded good and we ended up putting more than music together. We have done many shows together and have sung at many gatherings and church functions. I introduced him to Mom, and when Nolan said, "Hello, Mrs. Zappa," Mom looked up at him, as Mom was four-foot-eleven and Nolan was six-foot-tall, and said, "My name is Rose Marie!" I said, "That's it, you're in!" We all had a wonderful relationship, Mom and Nolan and Carl getting to know each other. My kids loved him, his Mom loved me, gee, and it was a family affair! We married in 2007, and I know that all my family, Frank, Dad, Mom, and Nolan's dad, they all approved.

In 2002, I was flown to Bad Doberan, Germany for the Zappanale, a three-day outdoor festival of the celebration of Frank's music played by bands from all over the world. My brother Bob was also there, as was Ed Palermo and his 18-piece band. I reconnected with Ike Willis, the late Jimmy Carl Black and met his wife Moni. I also met Napoleon Brock, Scott Thunes and many other Zappa alumni that were all playing and singing excellently. I performed with Ed's band and had an incredible time there. Wolfhard Kutz was our host, and he started the whole thing two decades before. It was a most memorable time for me, and they also dedicated a bust of Frank in the park in the city. The bust was placed at the point where the road splits and goes to the left and right as you enter the city. The people there were so wonderful to Bob and me. We were interviewed on local Bad Doberan television and I also did a radio interview. We were also taken to the city hall that was really ornate and quite beautiful. When I was in the park at the dedication, I was asked to have my picture taken with many of the locals and it was great fun. Taking the stage that evening, I had my camera with me, and I stated that since everyone had taken pictures of me, now it was my turn to take pictures of them! I got some great pictures of the crowd waving at me, and there were about 3,500 people there.

Thanksgiving Day 2003 was going to be a great day. We were taking Carl and Mom over to Nolan's Aunt Bessie's house to meet the rest of Nolan's family. I called Mom to see how she was, and she informed me that she was all dressed and ready to go. About 20 minutes later, Carl called saying that Mom had fallen and to come over. Nolan and I dashed over and found Mom lying on her left side. We sat her up and asked her if she was all right and if she could move her leg. She looked shaken and her leg was immobile. We called the ambulance and headed for the hospital. Her hip was broken and she had surgery. I pretty much lived there while she convalesced. After two months of care, physical therapy and pain, she was coming to the end. Carl called me at 3:30 AM on Monday, January 18th, saying that Mom was sick and wanted me. I went over and stayed with her. She slept all the rest of the day on Monday and Tuesday morning, and she wasn't any better. I took her to the hospital, a journey that was made over 20 times from 1999 to 2004. This time, however, was to be her last journey. For the next eight days, she was in the hospital and it was touch and go, but by Wednesday of the following week, she was taken to a convalescent home in Burbank for, what the doctor called, "comfort care." It was her time to go home. My daughter Eva, my friend Shirley and I were there, and after we sang "You Are My Sunshine" to her, I held Mom's hand as she passed away. I know she was happy to go; she had no problem with it. That's just the way Mom was. She was a responsible person, responsible for her life and her dignified passing. She was so elegant, always concerned for her family and not wanting anyone to be sad for her. I miss her so much. This all happened because Mom fell on Thanksgiving Day, and like the domino theory, it all fell down and ended when the last domino fell.

Above: me and Mom in 1998.

Nolan came to the hospital, too late to say goodbye, but he was there as the priest and all of us held hands and sent her off with prayers and love. I know Dad, Frank and her sister Mary were three of the many friends and relatives that were waiting for her. What a homecoming that must have been.

Mari Linville took this great photo of Nolan and me!

NOT "THE IDLE MEANDERINGS OF A CHEMICALLY ALTERED IMAGINATION"

Frank was a formidable presence in life, and I'm sure, in afterlife. I've had the honor of being aware of both times. Whether I was a child, bubblegummer or adult, Frank played in a large portion of my life. When I was a little girl, I wanted to be around Frank all the time. His age, his friends and sometimes my dad kept me apart from him. When I was a young girl, I wanted to be like Frank, tall and funny like he was. When he began his life of a musician/artist/composer/guitarist, his life kept us apart sometimes. There was always something to keep Frank and me apart: time, circumstance and other family members. But it's like lifelong friends — they know they love each other, and down deep, know they will be together eventually. I thought of Frank always when he got sick with prostate cancer and prayed hard for him to survive and be healed. I don't think he wanted to exist with cancer; it would cut into his work time. Healed? Yes, in the big picture of it all, he was healed, perfectly and eternally. Frank was not the weirdo, crazed person some people thought he was. He was, as I said earlier, very protective of his family. When I was thirty, I went over to see him and I wore a shirt that read, "My Body Belongs To Me…But I Share." He looked at it and said, "You're not one of those girls that rolls around on the floor are you?" "Sure!" I said, jokingly. He just groaned. He would look at stuff and be disgusted with it, like a friend had found an ad in the paper for a sex aid and he looked at it and just grimaced and turned away. The harshness of some of his lyrics was for shock value and I doubt that he would really do some of the things he sang about. But hey, what do I know! Frank was full of surprises! Even after he died.

While I lived in Las Vegas, I lived with a good friend of mine, Michelle Dean, who I worked together with on the psychic line. Misha is clairaudient, which means she can hear what the dear departed say. One day, after I had moved to Vegas, we were sitting in her room talking, and she suddenly stopped and said, "Frank's here." I said, "What do you mean 'Frank's here'?" "Just what I said, Frank is here." She then proceeded to tell me what she heard Frank saying to her. I never told Misha about the three-page letter I sent Frank before he died, the videotape of me singing and a cassette of a song I wrote, recorded and sang. She told me that he kept the letter on his desk and looked at it a lot, and then she saw him hold up the videotape and the cassette. I asked him if he was mad at me because I never got a response to the things I sent him. He said he had been too sick to talk to anyone, but that he, and he emphasized this, loved his little sister. Whenever we would call to talk to him, he was either getting a massage, sleeping or whatever it was, but we couldn't talk to him. It was still hard to not be able to talk to him and comfort him. Another day, I had written a poem to Frank and it was really good, if I do say so myself! A few days later, I went through all of my papers and couldn't find it at all. I asked Misha if Frank knew where it was. She got quiet and then started laughing; she said he was waving it at her. So much for not being able to take it with you! Another time, we were sitting in her room talking, and all of a sudden, the sound of the washing machine lid slammed down. I went to look and it was in an upright position; it hadn't come down. That apartment was a very busy place. I feel that a lot of the things that have happened in my life have been influenced by Frank when he was here, and now that he's over "there," wherever "there" is. I am very happy that most of the people I meet know who Frank is and love him and his music. Some of them recite whole album lyrics to me! I have heard some people say that they can't start their day without cranking Frank in the morning. Some use coffee, others use Frank!

I hope that you have enjoyed, and maybe now understand, my family and me a little more, and even if you don't, hey, it was a hell of a ride! Thank you for your time.

FRANK ZAPPA
"ABSTRACT SELF-PORTRAIT"

Only Frank and God knew what was going on in Frank's mind when he painted "ABSTRACT SELF-PORTRAIT." This was a gift to me from Frank many decades ago, so I imagine it was painted when he was in his late teens or early twenties.

I was always fascinated by it: the sad, tortured look in the eyes of the painting. Some look at it and see two faces in it — I only see one face. Art is in the eye of the beholder, I guess.

Frank's artistic expression with oil on canvas stemmed from many bedridden weekends, as a youngster, suffering with asthma. Mom would bring him toys and things to draw with. His puppetry work also stemmed from that time. Frank had a fertile imagination, as evidenced by his massive body of music work. As a teen, he went through a phase of frustration at a lack of things to do and places to go, in 1950s Lancaster, California. As he dabbled in drums, guitar, artwork and girls, soon his personality became even more glaringly apparent in his art, be it music or canvas. When the Zappa family later moved back to Claremont while Frank lived in Ontario with his first wife Kay, that's when I believe this piece, "ABSTRACT SELF-PORTRAIT." was conceived and executed. Frank was a genuine talent – perhaps even genius. Not to mention, he was a wonderful brother. I treasure the bond I had with him as my brother and as a fellow artist.

MORE TRIVIAL POOP OR LIFE AFTER FRANK

This book has been very therapeutic for me, and it's been 18 years since it was first printed. It almost didn't get reprinted, but that's another story. That may be another book in itself!

Lots of life has happened since then.

In the spring of 2003, I received a large box containing the fruit of my writing…the first book. I had several book signings. In April, I went to New York for a book signing and Connecticut for a radio show. It was my first time ever taking the Long Island Ferry. Of course, it didn't help that I had a raging fever and cold! In September, I had a signing in Rancho Cucamonga, CA (where Frank's notorious Studio Z was on Archibald Avenue), and at that signing, an old school mate of mine, Joan Balisz, from Pomona Catholic Girls High School, was there. It is always great when friends from the past show up and make the whole scene worthwhile. Then we went to our previous home in Lancaster, California, and at that one, my husband Nolan Porter, mother Rose Marie Zappa and brother Carl Zappa were also there. I was really excited that my mother and brother came along; it really was a family affair that day! My book had four signatures that time, and anyone who has my book with all four signatures has a real collector's item that was put on eBay the next day! It was also there that I met a now good friend and major fan of Frank's, Lou Allred. He holds his yearly, infamous "Day In The Desert" at his place in Lancaster. At one particular event, many fans of Frank's came out to hear Zappa alumni Denny Walley, the original Blackouts (Peter Lovio, Wally Salazar and Johnny Franklin), the late bassist Tom Leavey (not from Frank's band, but from Jimmy Carl Black's group Geronimo Black), and Jim "Motorhead" Sherwood, also from Frank's band, to jam with me, and of course Nolan, and other people there who wanted to sing. For the first event held in 2001, my brother Carl was also there and signed sweat socks for everyone. Also on that day, while I was sitting and enjoying the banter and laughter, a very distinguished, handsome black man came up to me and said, "Are you Candy?" I said "yes" and he said, "I'm Johnny Franklin!" I was so excited to meet him again. I was seven the last time I saw him with Peter Lovio and Wally Salazar.

Lou Allred has one of the biggest collections of Frank's memorabilia I've ever seen; wall-to-wall to ceiling pictures, videos, etc. There were over 200 people the last time we held a concert, some of which were fellow high school graduates of Frank's. It was nice to meet them and hear their stories of Frank's antics in high school. It's like being there. Hey wait, I was there! Well, I was only seven years old, but I remember on graduation night in June 1958 watching Frank walk across the stage holding up his diploma like a badge of honor! It was like he was saying, "Hey look, they graduated me anyway!" The school wanted him out, so no matter what his grades were, he was graduated!

The last signing was at Borders Book Store in Westwood, California, in May 2003. Ironically, this Borders was near where Frank was buried at Westwood Cemetery. We also had a band, as Nolan and I performed some of Frank's tunes and a couple of others. Another quick story: when I was in New York, Manhattan to be exact, at B.B. King's to be even more exact, that night, Project/Object was playing. I got to do a few songs with those great guys. What a talented band they are. Also, I brought a copy of my book, and while we were sitting backstage, Don Preston was thumbing through it. He came over to me and he said, "Can I ask you a question?" I said sure. He went on, "Where were you in the '70s when we were touring? I'm sorry I honestly didn't know Frank had a sister." So, I told him I was raising kids and married, and now you know he has a sister and don't forget it! I heard that a lot through the years that people didn't know Frank had a sister. That's why I wrote the book, to let everyone know that yes Frank had a mom, dad, two other brothers and two sisters (me and Ann)! That night at the Borders signing, my mother Rose Marie attended, and that was the first and sadly, the last time she ever saw us perform.

My mom Rose Marie had her 90th birthday on June 7th and it was a great day. I had a friend of Nolan's, Timothy Nicely, videotape the party and I am glad I did that. My sister Ann Zappa flew out from North Carolina, and her son Brooks, my three children, David, Julie and Eva, my brother Carl and his friend Jerry were in attendance. It was a big day for Mom: food, cake, lots of memories of our family and Mom making a wish. After we all blew the candles out for her, she made her wish, which was "I wish I could live to be 91." How prophetic.

In March of 2004, I went back to work. During this time Nolan and I were deciding to move in together and I knew I didn't want to live in North Hollywood. There were too many Mom memories that made me sad. I am just now able to drive around there without being really sad. That hurt takes a while to get over; in fact, I don't think you really ever get over it. Like a sore, you put ointment and a band-aid on it. It heals, but it sometimes leaves a scar to remind you.

We were able to find a place to live in Los Angeles, and in November of 2004, Nolan and I were officially bunk buddies. Thank goodness for the help we had moving. One week later, I was laid off from my work, as it was a temporary gig. Figures, doesn't it? Just when things looked really good, making good money, a new start — the rug gets yanked right out from under us. Our first year was tight money-wise, but we weathered it. It was quite an adjustment for Nolan, who had lived alone for 16 years.

2005 came in with a bang: new jobs for Nolan and me, my passing of a kidney stone, getting very sick with a throat virus and surviving it all. We also performed a show with a lawyer/songwriter, and it was quite successful. My relationship with Nolan was getting really good, much steadier.

In 2006, a friend forwarded an e-mail from someone in Wales, asking if Nolan Porter was alive. I responded that yes, he was indeed alive and well and living with me. Negotiations went back and forth, and eventually we were flown to Wales in March for Nolan to perform three of his songs from his album "Nolan." He is still very popular in England and Wales for "Northern Soul" events. It was an experience we will never forget. They really know how to party there! As with the good, sad things happen too. My mother's sister Fifi, who was 101 years old and a good friend Rosalie Nakano, passed away that year. I was also let go from the job I was working at. They say things happen in threes.

In 2007, there was another troop movement to the San Fernando Valley, and in April of that year, Nolan made an honest woman out of me and we married in an Elvis chapel in Las Vegas, but the minister who married us wasn't an Elvis impersonator. It was the best time we ever had in Vegas, and we won a little cash too. Later that year in July, I went back to work!

2008 went by quickly, but I lost another friend: Lou Allred's wife, Karen. In November, I was laid off again. Sometimes the months just fly by, people go, things happen and all of a sudden it's...2009 and my daughter Eva had a little girl, Michael Jackson, Farrah Fawcett and Billy Mays died. I had surgery on my right arm, and on Halloween my daughter and her man Frank got married in Las Vegas. Sort of a trend, don't ya think?

On January 16, 2010, I lost a long time-friend, Vicki Mahoney. That same week, I had to put another long-time friend and kitty named Frankie (guess who he's named after?) to sleep. I miss him so much. When they brought him in for me to say goodbye (my most unfavorite word in the English language), I whispered in his ear to make sure to find Frank so he could be with him. That following Monday, it was a rainy, dreary day and I crawled back to bed so depressed. I fell asleep and had a dream that he jumped up on the bed and looked at me as if to say, "What's the big deal, I'm still here!" Nolan and I heard him and felt his presence.

As of late, we haven't heard him at all or felt his presence. On April 22, 2011, while sitting at my computer, I heard the plaintive wailing of a tiny kitten and I went to investigate. There was a tiny, and I mean tiny (he fit in my small hand) gray fur ball of a kitty crying and peeing all over the place. I picked him up (I assumed it was a he) and my neighbor Jeff took me to the pet store, where I purchased a little bottle and kitty milk. I guessed his age at about two weeks. I nursed him with the bottle for four weeks and then weaned him to wet and dry food and water. He is now three times the size he was when I first found him. I call him Chewie, as he likes to chew on my hands! I look like a patchwork quilt with all the scratches on my hands and legs! He is exhibiting characteristics of Frankie, which I find quite amusing. Do animals reincarnate?

My children are always a source of great joy to me and are all good and successful adults. I was reintroduced to my 17-year-old grandson Damian at my 60th birthday party in March 2011. What a handsome young man he is! I have not seen him since he was three. My husband Nolan has been a great source of fun, support, laughter and common sense to me when I sometimes don't exhibit common sense, which isn't often, but it does happen occasionally.

My album "...To Be Perfectly Frank..." was released on July 27, 2011, and both of Nolan's albums ("No Apologies" and "Nolan") came out two days later. All three were released on our Porterville Records label. We're absolutely thrilled to be part of the wonderful world of digital music!

On August 14, 2011, the longest living original resident of Oak Park Drive in Claremont, California, Mrs. Edith Henrietta Ewing, passed on at 95. She outlived her husband, Bill, and three sons, Bill, Jeff and her oldest son, whose name I didn't know. Edie was the neighborhood watchguard and she knew everyone, where they came from, and never had a bad word to say about anyone. She was loved by so many people and she cared about everyone she met. After my mother passed in 2004, I kept up with her. Nolan and I and sometimes Nolan's mom Estelle would visit her after church and bring her favorite lunch, Kentucky Fried Chicken! Edie had a hearty appetite even in her nineties and she loved music. Every time I called her, she would sing "You Must Have Been A Beautiful Baby." When my dad had his heart attack in 1958, Edie would take care of me after school while Mom went to the hospital to visit Dad. She would fix my favorite chocolate milk and a snack, and then walk me home across the street and talk with Mom about how Dad was doing. When my dad wouldn't let me watch "The Twilight Zone," I would go over to Edie's and we would watch it with her son Billy. Their house was like a haven to me and I loved to visit with them. Edie, you were loved and will be missed.

I have made a new friend too, Larry Rogak. He is a lawyer in New York. My brother Bob sent me an interview that Larry did with Frank over 30 years ago and I was introduced to him. Larry also has a great picture with Frank here in the book. We became immediate friends, e-mailing almost every day with jokes, witty remarks and stories. Nice to have a lawyer as a friend!

I am also on Facebook, a marvelous place to network. I have made so many friends and connected with my cousin Debbie Zappa Katz. We haven't seen each other in 21 years and she found me! Also, not to mention other friends I haven't heard from in years — they found me too. Just about everyone on my "friends" page is a fan of Frank's and it's wonderful to have them as friends. Some other things that have come to mind and/or have happened recently:

I guess some of you might wonder how I feel about being related to Frank Zappa, growing up with him, knowing him, and I do tell about it in this book. There were times, after he passed, that I couldn't listen to his music or even read anything about him, it was just too painful. A friend asked me how I felt about being Frank's sister, and I told her it felt pretty damn good. Fans look at him from a different perspective than me, my other brothers, and even my parents before they passed. I'm sure that they must have worked it all out by now, all of them being together now. I'm not too sure how Gail is reacting to it all, but my folks were always cordial to her, even in Gail's not so cordial moods.

Whenever Frank would visit us, after he had moved out, it was like Christmas to me - so exciting - because I knew Frank would have a surprise to tell us and regale us with his exploits. He met so many famous people, and to him, it was just an average day. But to me, oh, it was like being in the same room with them. He told us about how he met Burt Ward, Robin in the "Batman" series. Evidently, Burt and Adam West couldn't stand each other! I thought that was intriguing. He met Andy Griffith and The Byrds. He met so many people that it was like eating a hot fudge sundae with nuts!

I also mentioned that one night, Frank and Don Van Vliet, aka Captain Beefheart, came over to the house and listened to me play my guitar and sing a song. I was happy that they both liked the song and my voice. It's nice to be verified! Frank is still an inspiration to me, to write, sing and get to work!

I went to a concert of Frank's one time at Cal Poly Los Angeles and I had arranged with Frank for us to see him backstage. When I got backstage, they wouldn't let me in and wouldn't get anyone backstage that I knew to come and talk to me. I called Frank the next day and told him what happened, and his response was, "Well, we have the people there to keep out the riff raff." Ha! Real funny, Frank! That made me feel real special. I have attended many concerts, and all were amazing and really incredible. As I listen to the music, I have to say that I've never heard anything like it before, during or since. Frank was a genius, a maestro composer/conductor and businessman. How do you top that?

When we were growing up with Frank being eleven years older than me, he hung out with his friends and I wasn't allowed to be around them. Dad was very protective. But that doesn't matter - I've gotten to meet them all over again as an adult. I was only six when we lived in Lancaster. I was sheltered from a lot of stuff as a kid, but I loved Frank very much and knew there was something about him, even when I was a kid.

I remember the boys playing touch football in the backyard of our Lancaster house. I wanted to play too, being a little tomgirl. I also remember my dad standing at the back door admonishing the boys to watch out for their sister. Oh, whoa be to him who let me get hurt! We also had a big Doughboy swimming pool in the backyard. I remember trying to get in and my brother Bob telling me to come and sit on the inner tube he was sitting on. I slipped and wound up at the bottom of the pool! I was choking and gasping for air and I got out of that pool in a hurry!

That was also the time mom took me and Carl to Baltimore, Maryland for her mother's funeral. It was the first time I was on a prop job and I was so nauseated. The funeral itself was so surreal to both Carl and me. We didn't understand what was going on, so we giggled - nervous giggling - and then we were invited to step up and see grandma in her coffin….dead….cold….yikes! I touched her and she was hard. How the hell does a six-year-old girl process this to make any sense? Our Aunt Fifi gave Carl and me a nickel each to sit still and be quiet. Good parenting skills! Our trip on the way home went like this: we had to take the bus home as it snowed so bad, the plane had to land, and we got stuck in the Texas Panhandle. We ended up staying overnight in a school auditorium. Mom was a total saint, and she should be nominated for sainthood for all she did for us. She took it all in stride, and I know she wasn't thrilled with the situation.

Another thing that happened in Lancaster. One morning, Carl and I were awakened early and taken to the hospital under the guise of going on a trip. We went on a trip alright - a trip to the hospital to have our tonsils taken out! Mom was always so afraid about my reaction to doctors, and especially needles. How ironic, as I inject myself nightly with insulin…When I got into the prep room, they wanted to give me a shot to calm me down. I screamed like I was being murdered, and that really must have unnerved my parents as well as the nurses and doctors! After they brought me in the operating room, I woke up and saw a man with a mask and horn-rimmed glasses leaning over me and he said, "She's awake!" So, they put the ether mask back on my face as I tried to fend them off! I got my mom back, though. I made her stay overnight with me on a cot the nurses put in our room. To placate us, Carl and I received ice cream and toys.

Mom was the mildest mannered woman I ever knew, and I think a lot of her ways rubbed off on me. I know when I look in the mirror, I see her in my face. Every once in a while, she'd come up with an expression that would make do a double take. There was someone, I can't remember who it was, but she said of him, "He should live, but not make it a habit." I laughed pretty hard at that. My dad knew what he was doing when he married her. She put up with so much stuff from all of us. I think when Frank became famous, both mom and dad might not have thought it would happen… and then it did. Frank was so jazzed when his first album came out, and he wanted his family's approval so much. You might not think wouldn't care, but he did, as in my story of him coming to the house on Palo Verde in Montclair, CA. He brought his album into the house and put it on our little record player, and as we all listened to "Wowie Zowie" and "Hungry Freaks Daddy," "Who Are The Brain Police?" came on next and we kind of stopped what we were doing. Hearing "I think I'm gonna die" over and over again was a little unnerving, but then Frank smiled big and said, "Isn't this great?" Yes, Frank, it was totally bitchen!

My dad was an interesting man. His life wasn't easy as a child. Even as a young man, he ran into challenges - a couple were him being an Italian, and another, being Catholic. Even though, he did his best in college and after he married and produced five children. My sister Ann was a product of his previous marriage. My earliest memories of dad were of him sitting in the living room reading the paper and watching his beloved cowboy and pirate movies. It was something I think he secretly wished he could have been - either a cowboy or a pirate. I mean, hey, we all have our fantasies. I used to have to get up early on Saturday mornings to watch my cartoons, but somehow he would always beat me to the television and some cowboy movie would be blasting away…

When I was about eight, he would take me with him to the store where he would lavishly look at the fruits, meats and vegetables. As a boy, all his family would have to eat was pasta. Not having things makes you appreciate having them. Then, he would hold out his hand with pennies and nickels and tell me to take what I wanted to so I could buy a sweet. In those days, a nickel would buy a lot of candy! Dad would also buy exotic things like pig's feet, tripe and smoked fish, and I was the only one of the kids who would sit and eat those with him. He must have loved that his little girl liked the odd things along with him. You could see mom running the other way…
He was also diabetic, the thing that eventually took his life. Mom said she could always tell when he would go in the kitchen as she would make a pie, and part of the crust would be missing. Dad would sneak a piece. He used to tell me, in his later years, that his hands would be numb - from poor circulation - and there were days when he just did not feel good. I can relate to both, adding in neuropathy in my feet.

His relationship with Frank was, from my view, fairly strained. I think when we were all kids, it was easier to deal with us, but as any parent can tell you, once your child learns to talk and think, it's pretty much a done deal. Frank did both and more; he thought, talked, did his own thing, made his own rules and rebelled against dad and anyone who tried to bend him their way. It made me sad. One day, I told a friend of mine that I didn't think my dad liked my brother, as that was how it seemed. Mom told me one time, Frank had some of his friends over to the house on Oak Park Drive in Claremont and they were playing music and dancing. Dad came home from work and saw Frank dancing with mom. He wasn't too happy about it and sort of told mom something like, "It's me or him." I know that sounds odd, but there was a certain power play between dad and Frank.

I think once Frank became famous and dad heard some of Frank's music, things calmed down with them. The concert that dad and I went to when Frank had Flo and Eddie with them was an eye-opener for dad. We were introduced to a lovely aroma of pot, and he got to brag to the man sitting next to him. He pointed at Frank and told the man, "That's my son!"

In 2003, I was introduced to a gentleman by the name of Art Utnehmer. He was in the process of making an indie film named "FOOSBALL: The Movie," a touching love story about a boy and his Foosball game and the several other dicey characters in the movie! Of course, I was one of them. Art and I clicked instantly and he asked me to play Electra, the mother of two of the main characters. I'm not a professional actress, but even with an "I'm not sure I should do this" feeling, I said OK. It was an experience I won't forget and we had a ball filming it. I met some very interesting people during the during the course of the shooting. "FOOSBALL: The Movie" finally debuted at The Screening Room in Tucson, Arizona on November 17, 2010!

In 2015, I was asked to sing a couple of songs on my friend Ed Palermo's latest album, "One Child Left Behind." I recorded one of Frank's songs, "Evelyn, A Modified Dog," and a song by Los Lobos: "Kiko And The Lavender Moon." I had a blast, and of course, Ed's musicians always make me sound good!

Wishes do come true, and in July 2016, both Nolan and I were flown again to Hamburg to attend the Zappanale in Bad Doberan. The weather was cold, rainy and windy - just like I like it, but not being out in it! Nolan and I opened the festival with Denny Walley and The Muffin Men, and it was a great festival from there on! I was explaining to the audience that a lot of things had transpired since my first appearance in 2002. I had written a book, and my second edition was there at the festival. My mother passed away and I married a man of color. I said, "In fact, you may know him, Mr. Nolan Porter!" Evidently, they did know him as the cheering was loud and friendly! We performed Nolan's song "If I Could Only Be Sure." I also sang with Z.E.R.O., another Zappa tribute band. There were about 4,000 people there, maybe more - I didn't take a head count…I also received a small three-legged stool, with the Zappanale logo hand carved on it, by this wonderful man who did fantastic wood work. It was an awesome four days, and we met so many great people.

We also met Paul Green and his School Of Rock. His students were incredible. Anyone who thinks Frank isn't relevant today is sadly mistaken. These young people were accomplished musicians and enjoyed playing Frank's music. I think that one of the nicest things for me during this visit was getting to know Denny Walley better, along with his wife Janet. I didn't realize that Denny was around when we lived in Lancaster. I was 6. He told me that he was friends with my brother Bob before he worked with Frank. Of course, Bunk Gardner and Don Preston were there and as fabulous as ever. We took lots of pictures.

Another wonderful thing happened on September 25, 2016. Nolan and I flew to New York and visited my brother Bob and his wife Diane in their Manhattan apartment. I hadn't seen Bob in 12 years, and his first wife Marcia had passed in 2013 from pancreatic cancer. Greg Russo, my publisher and good friend, was our chauffeur for the time we were there and drove us into Manhattan to visit them. Bob made his famous linguine and clam sauce. The conversation was lively, but it then turned to Frank's death and whether or not he was cremated. Bob was suffering from a disease called amyloidosis. It is a rare disease that occurs when an abnormal protein, called an amyloid, builds up in your organs and interferes with normal function. It was sad to see a man, who was once a Marine, turn into a 120-pound man who had trouble standing as the disease made him wobbly. Three weeks before he passed, he emailed me to have myself checked. I carry the mutant T3 gene, but all my tests came back normal. When I gave Bob a kiss on the cheek, little did I know that was the last time I'd see him. Bob passed away on December 8, 2018.

I've been asked a few times about the feud among Frank's kids, and I really have no answer except to say that Gail really made a mess of things and it's spilled over to her kids. Why didn't she give them each 25% instead of

20%/20%/30%/30%? That would've seemed the fair way to go. They should all have a say in the ZFT affairs - it's all of theirs anyway. I just hope they can mend the rift before too long. Families shouldn't fight. I mean, can't we all just get along?

There are many projects (like my album and other things on www.crossfirepublications.com) in the near future and I hope that you will attend, listen to, or read one of them. We are in the process of making an animated project which has been presented to a network. I will be doing the voice for one the characters. Thanks for your support over the years. It's always a pleasure to meet new friends and fans of Frank's. Any fan of Frank's is a friend of mine!

MOST RECENTLY...

I started working at an air conditioning company at the start of June 2017. It was fun going to work. My office mate Lucy had me in stitches laughing all day. When the phone would ring we'd laugh and say, "Hey, can't you see I'm having fun here?" I mean, who wants to take an order when there's stuff to laugh at? We got things done, but we had fun doing it.

Nolan's touring in the UK had been going on steadily: 2010, 2012, 2014, 2016, and then 2018. This year was, in my humble opinion, the best year as I joined Nolan in Blackpool, UK. We were flown there and stayed at the Biltmore across from the Irish Sea. It was just fabulous! A big "thank you" to Richard Searling for making it possible. We landed at Heathrow and were driven to our destination, where we took the first day to rest. We had dinner, watched television and had a much needed sleep. The next day, we went to the venue and rehearsed Nolan's songs with the band and the three background singers. I was fortunate enough to get to be on stage with them to sing and I loved it. Walking around the whole area of shops and the Blackpool venue, Winter Gardens, was superb. Nolan was stopped and asked to pose for pictures and his autograph on all sorts of items, from programs to hats, shirts, bags, etc. There were so many stands with merchandise of different artists, and we had Nolan's shirts too.

The other artists there with Nolan, the night of the performance, were Ann Sexton, Margie Joseph, Eloise Laws, and Patti Austin. The ladies got some nice love and applause but when Nolan came on stage, it was incredible. The audience cheered, screamed, applauded and generally went nuts! Nolan was so humbled by it, he felt overwhelmed! I had a terrific time talking with the other ladies backstage and learning about their lives. That was a great night. After the performance, we went upstairs and found a table and we all sat down to watch the dancers and hear the DJs spin records. That place was packed! The dancers were fabulous and very innovative, and the outfits were clear out of the '60s. We got back to the hotel and got more sleep.

In the middle of the night, I heard Nolan calling my name, quite adamantly. I got up to see what was wrong and he was in the bathroom having his first bout with vertigo. He said he'd been throwing up and was really dizzy. I helped him back to bed and had him sit up and calm down. I showed him a trick I did when I felt a bout with vertigo myself: sit straight up and turn your head slowly to the left and hold it for 10 seconds. Then, turn slowly back to center and slowly to the right, each time holding it for 10 seconds. He did that a few times and the vertigo seemed to calm down. I figured he needed to eat, so I went down to the restaurant and filled a plate with food. They put it on a tray for me, but it was kind of heavy. The manager offered to carry it upstairs to our room for me. I was so grateful and Nolan was too. That morning they were having a Q&A with some of the artists and Nolan was one of them. He couldn't do it though. He rested for the remainder of the day.

The next day we went to Winter Gardens and made our way to our booth being manned by Marie Gillespie. Many fans and looky-loos stopped by to purchase signed shirts and pose for pics with Nolan. We met so many lovely people. Most of them asked us to move to Blackpool! We even entertained the thought. As with all good things, they must come to an end. Back in the USA and back to work for us.

2019 took us to Bad Doberan, Germany for the Zappanale - my fourth one, Nolan's second. It was probably the best one. After settling into the hotel, we took the first day to rest and look around the little town.

It's such a beautiful place. The next day, we went through the park to see some music acts and have lunch. Then, it was off to the fairgrounds and the backstage tents. That year, they went vegan and the food was very interesting. The weather was cold, cloudy, and sprinkly. I was up first with Treacherous Cretins and we did "Uncle Remus" and "Cosmik Debris." At one point, Nolan and I were looking for some lunch, and after getting something to eat, we decided to park our butts on a picnic bench outside the tents. The sky was so dark and it was eerily calm. All of a sudden, the wind kicked up and lightning led to thunder and rain. We ran into the tent, but we were all promptly told to leave as the tents had electricity in them and they didn't want anyone to get zapped - no pun intended. The fairgrounds were right next to the Baltic Sea, so that place must have its own weather patterns. We found shelter in a wooden stall they used for horses. I was freezing, so our friend Jim Cohen ran to the tent and brought back my jacket. The stage where everyone was performing was flooded, so it had to be dried out before anyone could get back on it. Ed Palermo's Big Band came on next and I did a couple of tunes, "Let's Make The Water Turn Black" and "Directly From My Heart To You." That was the end of my singing for the night. Later, we all assembled on stage with the School Of Rock group and danced to the music.

Later on that year in October, Nolan left for the UK for another tour with a group called The Signatures. Gavin Creates-Webb arranged for Nolan to fly there and perform with the group. It was about this time I would see pictures of him performing, and he looked like he was swimming in his shirts. These were shirts he normally wore. Nolan was losing weight and looking so tired. He was doing what he loved.

In the year 2020, the shit hit the fan. Nolan would don his mask and gloves and head out to bring back boxes and bags of food, but no toilet paper. He was the hunter, taking care of us, braving the people out there. We used toilet paper sparingly until we could lay our hands on some. Nolan followed the news religiously night and day. We both stayed home protecting ourselves. I was cooking up a storm. We had so much food! Finally, in May my boss called and wondered if I was coming back to work. I did and Nolan did, too. It was also the start of our loved ones leaving us.

Two of my long time friends both died in June, five days apart. Both my brother Carl and sister Ann passed in November. It was also this time when Nolan became sick. After some consultation by medical staff, he was told he had a tumor on his liver and that it was advanced liver cancer. We discussed how his care would be, and he said he would go to a hospital. I told him that I would care for him. I was his twenty-four-seven nurse. This care for him started in late October and ended on February 4, 2021 at 8:15pm. It was the saddest thing I ever did, saying goodbye to my love, my heart and soul and telling him I would be okay and it was time to let go. My only comfort is knowing I will be with him and he'll be waiting for me when it's my time. We were married for 14 years and together for 22 years. Evidently, I am to go on and live my life by updating this book and writing my other book about Nolan and me called "If I Could Only Be Sure: The Life Of Nolan Porter." It will be available when this edition is ready.

PATRICE ZAPPA-PORTER
pattieford5@gmail.com

(Courtesy of photographer Melissa Wilson, with retouching by Eric Peterson and Greg Russo.)

Mom doing some shopping!

Mom, Carl and I at Knott's Berry Farm.

Dad

Carl at the front door!

Frank, Bob, and Carl.

At left: me and my guitar.

At right: my friends and I hanging out after "We're Only In It For The Money" was released in 1968.

Below: an FZ comic book!

Above left: It's time to hear a playback!

Above right: Posing with the first replica bust of Frank at Zappanale in 2002.

Below right: Ann Zappa in 2016.

At Zappanale 13.

Below: The September 27, 2016 summit at the famous Stop 20 Diner in Elmont, NY!
(left to right): Larry Rogak, Nolan, me, Carmen Pagán, Greg Russo.

I sang Frank's "Any Way The Wind Blows" with Z.E.R.O. (Zappa Early Renaissance Orchestra) at the Zappanale festival in 2016. That jacket looks great!

For a few years, Zappa fan Lou Allred displayed his amazing memorabilia collection with the attendance of former band associates at "Day In The Desert" gatherings. Below is an informal photo from the October 8, 2006 event assisted by former Blackouts/Omens member Peter Lovio.

(Back): Wally Salazar, me, Motorhead Sherwood, Denny Walley, Tom Leavey, John French, Doug Moon, Nolan.

(Front): Johnny Franklin, Lou Allred, Peter Lovio, Fred Salazar.

Above: That's me with Ike Willis at the Zappanale festival in Germany. When I got back to Hollywood, I performed with Project/Object and Ike at The Knitting Factory.

Below: I'm with Zappanale promoter Wolfhard Kutz.

From our first night together, that's me with my future husband Nolan Porter. We regularly performed together for more than two decades. Our "Once A Legacy" show featured a Frank Zappa tribute and appearances by other musicians with connections to FZ.

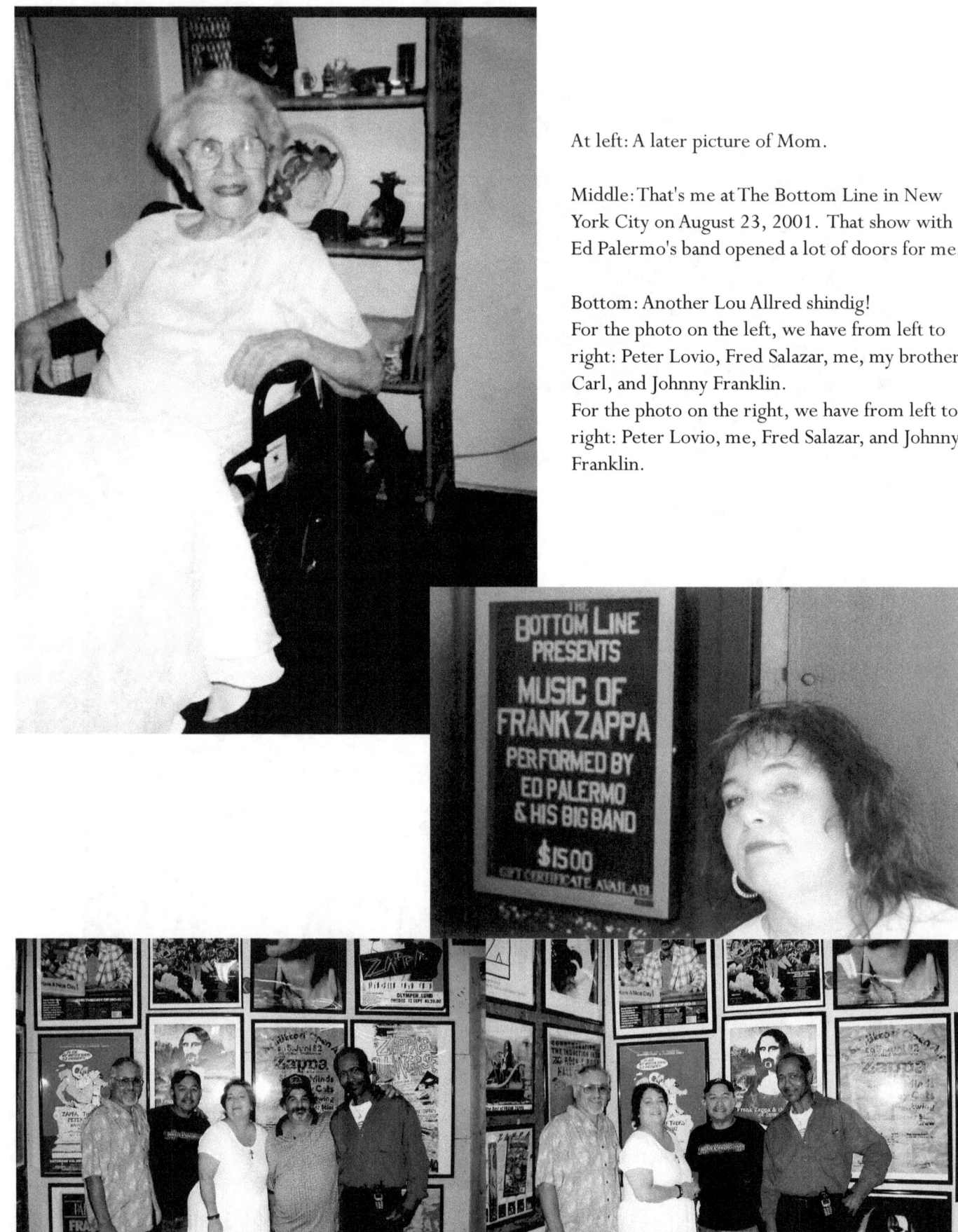

At left: A later picture of Mom.

Middle: That's me at The Bottom Line in New York City on August 23, 2001. That show with Ed Palermo's band opened a lot of doors for me.

Bottom: Another Lou Allred shindig!
For the photo on the left, we have from left to right: Peter Lovio, Fred Salazar, me, my brother Carl, and Johnny Franklin.
For the photo on the right, we have from left to right: Peter Lovio, me, Fred Salazar, and Johnny Franklin.

Above: Jimmy Carl Black and I at Zappanale 13.

Below: More wonderment at Zappanale 13, and check out Ed Palermo on sax in the back!

ON THIS PAGE: That's right - even more excitement from Zappanale 13! At the top, Ed Palermo is still behind me!
Below: I'm hanging with my brother Bob and Jimmy Carl Black at Zappanale 13.
ON THE NEXT PAGE: On top, Dr. Dot makes a house call in 2015!
In the middle is Armin Beck's photo of me on stage with The Muffin Men at Zappanale 27 in 2016.
On the bottom left, Armin and his friend Markus hang with me backstage at Zappanale 27.
On the bottom right, Armin joins Nolan and I for a great meal at Denny's!

THE PATRICE AND NOLAN SECTION!

RECOLLECTIONS OF FRANK ZAPPA

Mr. Zappa and I
by Alessandra Izzo

Since I was a young girl, I have been a music addict; it was my life. I loved music and musicians more than anything else. I went to concerts and used to spend hours studying English through American and English song texts. But at a certain point, something changed.

The first time I crashed into the music of Baltimore's great genius was around 1976-1977. I fell in love with Frank and his music at first sight. I had never heard something like that, until that moment. I was born and lived in Naples, Italy, and I was still a child when I knew the best moustache in the United States.

I decided I had to meet Frank Zappa in any possible way. And that was it.

It was the summer of 1982. In Naples there were two big concerts: The Rolling Stones and Frank Zappa. Since I was almost 18 years old, I thought: "This is my occasion." I started to work on the radio and the cameramen and I were able to meet my guru and mentor. With everything positive Mr. Zappa had taught me since I was a child, such as slipping out of my bad days in a soft way (I already was a rebel - a bit turbulent), I decided to be an artist.

I picked Frank Zappa as my "personal counselor" when I was 12 years old, and I noticed that I would have learned more from him than Jesus Christ. That was the time I threw myself into rock 'n' roll. I was cute: I had blonde hair at that time - I am a redhead now. I was also a late, hippie-dressed half-daughter of flowers and half punk - a girl of my generation.

After the concert in Rome, Frank walked by, drank a bit of Coke from my glass without my knowledge. It was something that he used to do with girls he liked. We promised to see each other one day in Naples, my home. I went to Rome, but the day after I went back home to see him again and listen to his music. Zappa loved to play famous songs in the city he was performing in, and in Naples he sang the 1977 hit "'na tazzulella 'e cafè" by Pino Daniele.

It had been love at first sight for me, and I have to say he could not get his eyes off of me. He came to me and told me, "You are very beautiful, but you are very young, right?" I answered shamelessly, my eyes wide open under a blonde side bangs: "I'm turning 18 in October." He was a gentleman.

After the concert we talked a lot. I loved his company. He had a strong charm: on one hand, he was free and easy, a funny songwriter (he used to call his texts "stupid songs"); on the other hand, he was serious, a fascinating composer who could make anyone feel uncomfortable with his black deep eyes. His look could kill: penetrating, sensual, but he could chill your blood. Anyway, he had always been sweet with me.

In July 1982, nothing hot happened, but after two or three years we saw each other in Viareggio, Tuscany, and then a sort of "special friendship" was born. I was honored that he looked for me just to have a chat. I was only 20 and he was 44, but we were at ease. We talked a lot. He was always curious to know if I was happy and peaceful, which were my life's goals. It was like we had known each other forever.

I obviously had a crush on him, and I think he liked me as well, even if he was happily married and had four children. I told him I moved to Rome to study acting and to become an actress. He was very stimulating and he kept on telling me not to give up even when hard times would have come. I had to think I would have made it.

He was humorous, but his behavior changed often because of the exhausting tours. Frank was always working or composing in his studio/basement in L.A. when he was not rehearsing. Yes, he was a workaholic. It seemed like work was his favorite word.

Zappa and I had been in touch until 1988, the last year I saw him. He was in Italy. He was more charming than ever, but very nervous, weak and weird. He delegated things to Scott Thunes (a real odd guy, completely full of himself), and he was strict and annoyed by his "Best Band." Frank was going out much less after the concerts, only to dine with his Italian booking agent (they seemed to get along real well). I understood he was changing, but nobody would have ever imagined, except for his family and a few musicians, that inside Frank was growing a cruel and silent beast that was slowly killing him.

In 1993, when Frank died, I had been in the States for the longest time in my life. I was a correspondent for a cinema TV show, and I had to interview actors, directors and rock stars. I was seduced by the idea of giving Frank a last goodbye. But if you were a woman - and a cute one too - Frank Zappa could be met anywhere, except in L.A.

Now, Frank was not only sick, but also he was not driving. He was at his house in L.A. with his wife Gail. For this reason, Frank was always at home or around with Gail and their children. It was impossible to see him. I had a mutual friend tell Frank that I was in town. Frank told him to say hi, and that he would have wanted to see me, and Miss No No (this was the nickname he gave me, but I will never tell the reason) made him happy, but he was…dying.

I often think about him and what he represented for me. I bless my life because I was able to meet him. Often, Frank Zappa is defined as an asshole, mean and self-centered, but it was not true. Frank defended himself, that was it. He was a fragile and vulnerable creature and he always tried to defend his person. He was simply a genius.

I shall remember him as one of the most brilliant people I met in my life - very deep and curious (in his "fake superficiality"). I was not only a fan; I was his pal.

Good luck Mr. Zappa, and I know you are still here to guide a part of us, as you like to do, and that we like it because you are always ahead of us.

Alessandra with her husband Dido.

Deborah Zappa Katz

Frank and I in 1974.

My husband Ed and I went to see Frank play at Merriweather Post Pavilion in August 1984 (the 30th). During the concert, a girl who was up dancing in the walkway/aisle took off her panties and threw them up on stage. So, Frank of course got silly with them during the performance. After the show, Ed and I went backstage. We hung out with Frank after he let in the entourage after about half an hour. A few minutes later, in comes one of the roadies with this girl (I wonder how she got backstage!). Now pantyless, this girl said she was dying to meet Frank. She started saying how she wanted a favor from him to get an autograph for a friend but how embarrassing it was to ask him for it. Frank, all of a sudden, got very serious, looked at her and said: "In the middle of a concert, after taking off your panties and throwing them on stage, what can be more embarrassing?" He gave the autograph and then the guy escorted her out. Frank always had a great sense of humor.

Debbie in front of the bust of Frank Zappa in Baltimore.

Ian Marek (down in France)

If you are the typical "sensible" music listener and you hear the first notes of the "Hot Rats" album for the first time, you are seriously knocked on your ass because this music has nothing at all in common with anything you have heard before or anything you will hear after. Such was the case with me. Zappa's music was exactly the sound I had been dreaming of, and there it was, just spinning there on the turntable like some Holy Grail. I experienced the same shock upon discovering "Freak Out!," "Over-Nite Sensation," "Roxy & Elsewhere" and so many other albums.

This is what I enjoyed the most about Zappa's music. There were always unique and different moments, like a perpetual surprise. It offered a completely imaginary world where you could meet strange people like The Grand Wazoo, Billy The Mountain, Greggery Peccary and many other "monsters." You could experience so many emotions with his music and all in a humorous way that flies in the face of our human condition. Frank Zappa was not talking about freedom; his art IS freedom! Anything, any time, anywhere, for no reason at all.

There are also those albums (like "The Grand Wazoo") that are so complex that they must be listened again and again to really understand the music. And if you make the effort to try, they really open doors in your mind for the rest of your life.

I can't recall the number of times I gave tapes to friends to make them discover this bizarre music. Most of the time, they had a positive reaction of surprise because the music can't leave you indifferent. I was glad to share it and I continue even today.

In the entire history of art there was only one Frank Zappa. We will probably have to wait 18,000 years or more to see such a personality again (zut alors!), but he left behind so much stuff that we can still discover more from him. He continues to be a major influence for me as a painter, musician and guitar player, and also in my general approach to life. Some of his words are a nice philosophy for all of us to follow, and they offer a very clear vision of our world. Definitely, he is an ideal brother for all of us, The Sons of Invention.

UNCLE FRANK
by Julie Waterman (Patrice's daughter)

I first met Frank when I was two, so I have no memory of that meeting. When I was 10, my brother David and sister Eva went to his house on Christmas Eve, stayed the night and had Christmas Day there. The majority of my visit involved playing with my cousins, but my brief meeting with Frank still burns in my mind's eye.

I was, of course, playing riotously when my mother called me over saying she "wanted me to meet somebody special." My mother glowed for her beloved brother to meet her children. Being a child of 10 as I was, my intuition was fully intact and uninhibited by the mundaneness of reality and I could see the man's aura, or was it his wild mane of hair?

I knew that he was extraordinary and it wasn't because I knew his music. At this point, he took us down into his studio and talked to us about the only thing he could have talked about - all of his music equipment and how he used it.

When I was 18, he sent me a cash birthday gift, and a month later, he passed away.

I have had visits with him in my dreams and they have always been happy and he even told me loved me. I believe if familial relations would have been allowed, I would have known my uncle more.

Perry Ostrin

I was at Candy's in-store reading at Borders in Westwood when "My Brother Was A Mother" was originally published. My picture with Frank comes from an event with Pierre Boulez and Robert Kraft at UCLA in 1989.

Christopher Lane (Tulsa, Oklahoma)

I was 17 when I first saw FZ in concert here in my home town of Tulsa, Oklahoma on October 18, 1980. This happened to be the night that the song "Hog Heaven" was recorded and later released on the "Shut Up 'N Play Yer Guitar" 3 LP set. All I can say is I was blessed to have been there and will always know in my heart that I was a part of that show. This was my first religious experience in the way of music. My life was changed forever after seeing both shows that night. I was lucky enough to see Frank the next year on October 14, 1981, but he unfortunately played one show although two were scheduled to be performed that night. The newspaper said the second show was canceled due to a lack of ticket sales, which was a bummer because I skipped school to be the first in line to assure myself front row seats for both shows! I still was able to get there and get all the way to the front row center stage. I was so excited to be so close to my new-found hero/ Li'l Stevie Vai was right in front of me with a shirt that read "Captain Kirk Fucks Aliens"! There has never been any music/musician that moves me like Frank's does, especially his guitar solos that to this day send shivers up my spine. Frank was so far ahead of his time and I was so sad the day I got the news he had passed. I know one day I will see him on the other side of the fence, and we will have lots to talk about! Frank was, and always will be, my hero and musical inspiration.

Top of next page: Christopher Lane's ticket stubs and two photos from the 1980 concert.

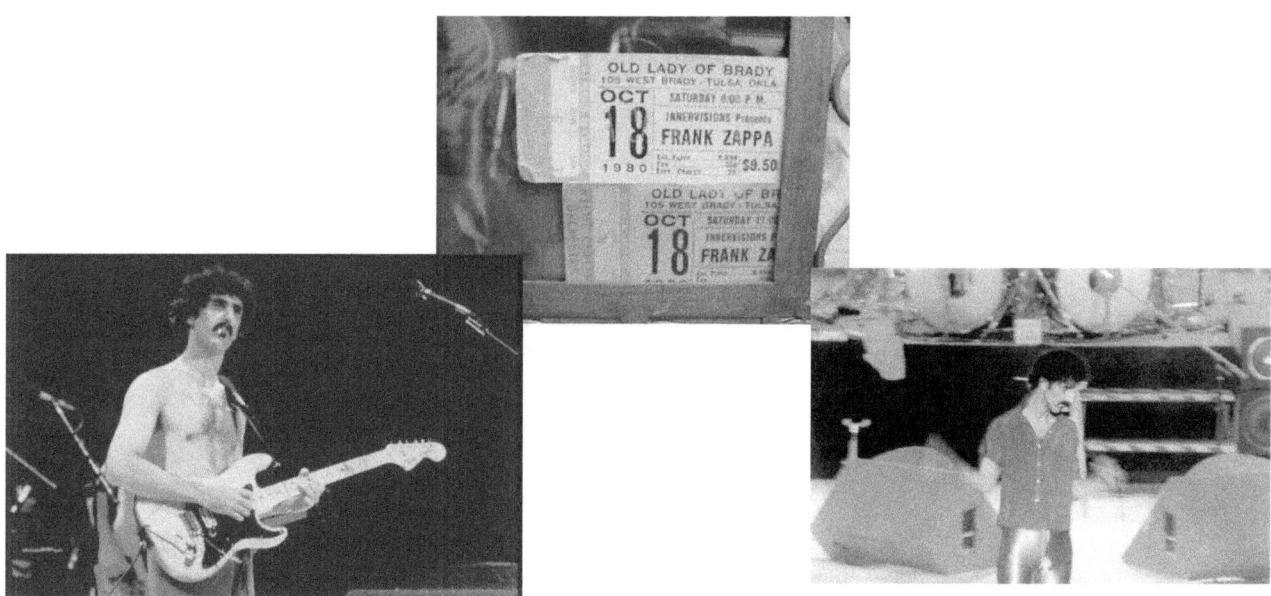

Glenn Leonard, the former Project/Object drummer who was at the helm of the band Pojama People until his untimely death in 2013, contributed his ticket stub from the 1981 Halloween show and a photo from the early show at The Tower Theatre in Upper Darby, Pennsylvania on April 29, 1980.

Jack Fecko

Brian Vincent

Kilissa Cissoko
(next page)

with FZ in 1981

How about a Frank Zappa tattoo?

This is the letter my friend Caroline Lambert and I wrote to Frank in 1981. He was gracious enough to write back. We were 17 and had a good laugh. But, Caroline was serious about wanting to open for Frank in Buffalo. Later on, in about 1997, we finally formed our own Zappa tribute band called The Voice Of Cheez. I hope you can find a place for this. We treasure it.

c/o Barking Pumpkin Records
PO Box 5510
Terre Haute Indiana
47805   8/25/81

Dear Frank,
 I don't know how to make a fab introduction to this letter, so I'll just get right to the point.
 My current fantasy is to ~~~~ perform in front of a huge audience. (Shea's stadium would be nice, but the Memorial aud. in Buffalo will do, ~~I guess~~).
 The word here is that you will be coming here sometime this fall and I would love to be your opening act, as it were. Just me — and I only want to do a few songs (Cilla Black, The Intergalactic Burnt Toast, etc...) You won't even have to pay me.
 All you have to do is ~~let me use your complete sound system~~. Let the security people there know that I'm supposed to be there so they don't kick me off of the stage or perform any violent acts on me and let me use your sound system.
 It would also be really gear if you could introduce me.
 I'm enclosing a self-addressed, stamped envelope to make it easier for you to respond. In fact, to make it even easier — my phone # is (716) 652-8173.

[margin: Just think, you could trade a name for yourself by being the one who introduced me to the world.]

[margin: love, "Caroline" "Com les Luminos" Lambert]

FRANK ZAPPA

October 5, 1981

Ms. Caroline Lambert
451 South Street
East Aurora, NY 14052

Dear Caroline:

It will not be possible for me to grant your request to perform in Buffalo. We never use any opening acts, or at least we haven't in the last five years. Also, the way our stage is set up it would be very inconvenient to have anyone else do anything on stage prior to our show.

Sorry I cannot help you, and thanks for your letter.

Yours truly,

Frank Zappa

FZ:sr

7720 SUNSET BLVD, LOS ANGELES, CA 90046 (213) 851-5461 TELEX 194738

Javier Marcote

From the archives of Frank's 1955-1956 Mission Bay High School yearbook comes the following:

Bobby Marquis (CKCU-FM, Ottawa, Ontario)

Since I began my research on Frank Zappa in 2009 for my radio show in Ottawa, Canada, I began to understand more about Frank the artist, and not Frank the freak. During my youth in the early '70s, the typical weekend house party consisted of music by CCR, Jimi Hendrix, The Doors, Grand Funk Railroad, and Zappa's "Freak Out!" album. At that time, most of my friends were doing acid, pot, hashish and alcohol. I was quite green and naive towards what they were doing for recreation, but I found out a lot about music: "It's a great way of Life." "Freak Out!" seemed to turn out at every house party thereafter. When I began my first year in high school in 1971, Zappa's album "The Mothers - Fillmore East '71" came out. As I listened to this somewhat risque type of performance, I went out and bought the album.

As time went on through my growing years, I managed to collect more Zappa albums. I found myself moving into other directions musically, with prog rock and studying classical music. When I got involved with radio at CKCU-FM off and on from 1988 to the present, "Joe's Garage" was a favorite among many DJs. It wasn't until I decided to research Frank Zappa that I found out how much of a genius he was, and how much I didn't know about him. Now I know what I've been missing.

Interviewing the Frank Zappa alumni on my radio program has also opened my eyes. Robert Martin, Ed Mann, Ike Willis, Tom Fowler and Don Preston have been so kind to me, and gave their precious time and stories, to make me understand who Frank Zappa is and was. To the alumni, I thank you. To Patrice Zappa-Porter, I'm so glad I had the chance to talk to you.

Below: Bobby Marquis' photos from a 1976 show in Ottawa, Ontario, Canada with Bianca. Also shown are a ticket stub from 1974, an article about a 1975 FZ concert in Ottawa, and the 1976 Canadian tour ad.

Listeners walk out as Zappa concert drones on

Ann Zappa

Ann Rives Zappa was born on November 20, 1931, in Durham, North Carolina. She is the daughter of Nelle Rives Cheek and Francis Vincent Zappa, Sr. After the divorce of her parents when she was four, she lived in Chatham County, North Carolina, with her mother, grandparents William Brooks Cheek and Rena Rives Cheek, and aunt Mabel Virginia Cheek. Ann was the great-granddaughter of Confederate Veterans David Edward Rives, Pvt., Co. E, 26th North Carolina Troops, and Noah Cheek, who served as a Private in the Confederate Infantry. She was a member of the Winnie Davis Chapter 259 of the United Daughters of the Confederacy.

She graduated from Needham Broughton High School in Raleigh in the Class of 1949. She attended Women's College (now the University of North Carolina at Greensboro) until her marriage to William Currier Cole in 1952. She was the mother of a daughter, Cynthia Anne Cole, and a son, William Brooks Cole.

Ann first met her stepmother Rose Marie Zappa when she was about ten. Her father and Rose Marie visited her in Chatham County. Frank was about three and Bobby was a baby. She thought her stepmother was beautiful and was astonished that Rose Marie was wearing riding pants. Over the years, Rose Marie was diligent in keeping in touch. When Cynthia was about four, Bill and Ann visited her father and family in Lancaster, California. She was fascinated with Frank, Bobby, Carl, and Patrice. She met the young woman who would become Frank's first wife.

When Ann was teaching in the Junior College in Chicago, she visited with Frank on three different occasions when he gave concerts there. She would visit with him in the afternoons, attend the sound check, and then enjoy his concerts. They shared family information. Ann was a great admirer of Frank's lyrics and told him once that he was a satirist on par with Jonathan Swift. Once in an interview, Gail Zappa denied the existence of another sister of Frank's.

Ann resided in Chatham County, North Carolina, on property where she was born and raised. She retired from a career as Head of the English Department at MacCormac Junior College, Chicago; and Administrative Assistant at the University of North Carolina at Chapel Hill.

Ann published two novels, "Time And Chance Happen To Them All" and "Fantasy Of A Gentleman." These stories were fictionalized life experiences and her characters were drawn from lives of friends. Her third and final book was "Memoirs of a Lady Cannoneer." This project was autobiographical, beginning in September 1997, with her first re-enactment of a historical battle that took place during the War Between the States. Ann was a member of Brunson's Battery, Pee Dee Light Artillery, and Kelly's Battery, Chesterfield Light Artillery and portrayed historical female artillery soldiers in living history presentations. She also belonged to several Southern historical organizations. Ann was a lifelong member of Lystra Baptist Church in Chatham County and was active in church work, singing in the Church Choir and serving as Church Clerk since 1988.

In the last two decades, Ann and Patrice became quite close. Both treasured having a sister and sharing family ties. Ann attended the wedding of Patrice and Nolan in Las Vegas, and she traveled to Las Vegas for the wedding of Eva Waterman and her husband Frank. In March 2011, Ann joined Patrice and family to celebrate Patrice's sixtieth birthday. Ann derived her devotion to family from two sources, Southern and Sicilian, and she was the older of two sisters of the late rock star, Frank Zappa. Ann passed away at her home in Chatham County, North Carolina on November 21, 2020, one day after her 89th birthday.

Larry Rogak
Backstage at the Palladium, NYC, Halloween 1981

One of the most memorable days of my life was May 8, 1980, the day I interviewed Frank Zappa at his suite in the St. Regis Hotel. I was a 22-year-old, second-year law student at the time. The following is a transcript — heretofore never published — of that interview. Being only 22 at the time, many of my questions are clumsy and/or naive — certainly not up to the level of a professional journalist. But I was just a fan, meeting my idol, and I don't think I had ever interviewed anybody about anything before.

I should also tell you that this transcript is unedited. Every word of the three-hour interview is in here. Unlike a magazine or other professional publisher, I have not omitted "stuff that might be boring," or otherwise chopped, channeled, lowered, louvered, or altered any of the content so as to make it fit between ads, or to satisfy the desires of some editor or publisher. It's all here, all raw.

And since this is a for-real interview, and an important historical record, I might as well tell you all that my real name is Larry Rogak and I am an attorney in New York. I'm also a writer. I write law books, and I also write comedy. If you go to Amazon.com and search my name, you'll find two very funny books I wrote that you'd probably enjoy: one is called "Haiku For Guys." The other is called "You Don't Know Dick." Trust me on this one: if you're a Frank Zappa fan, the edgy humor in these books will tickle your fancy all night long.

The original transcript of this interview was typed, by me, back in 1980, on a typewriter (any of you kids remember typewriters?).

I had a burning desire to meet Frank and I pondered for years about how to make it happen. It wasn't because of rock idol worship. It was because I had been reading and listening to Zappa interviews for years and Frank's philosophy and point of view totally grabbed me. It said to me: this guy makes sense. So my dream was to sit down with him and just talk about politics, people, and the world.

Inspiration hit me one day while I was in law school. One of my professors, during a lecture in Corporations class, quoted Frank as saying, "If you want to stop crime in America, put a policeman on every board of directors." The ol' light bulb turned on over my head. I had been following the story of Frank's suit against Warner Brothers for years. According to Frank, WB had taken four LPs worth of material from him and simply released it without his input, and without paying royalties. Might this be the shoehorn I could use to work my way into an interview?

I had been a contributor to my law school's newspaper. So on that pretext, I contacted Frank's press agent, Wartoke (the name and address of which was printed on the back of one of his albums) and made a pitch for an interview with Frank about his suit against WB. I sent Wartoke a letter - an actual paper letter through the U.S. Mail, which was the way letters were sent in 1980.

To my surprise, I actually got a call from them. Negotiations began, which centered around the concerns of Frank's lawyers about discussing pending litigation. Finally, I made this offer: Frank could edit the interview transcript before it was published. That sealed the deal.

I got a call telling me to meet Frank at the St. Regis Hotel on May 8. I owned a portable stereo cassette recorder – a rare item at the time – which I frequently employed in taping concerts I attended (for my own personal use, of course). So I appeared at the appointed place and time, with every hair on my body in goosebump mode. The door to the suite opened, and there stood John Smothers, in all his charming glory. He looked me over and I suppose I appeared harmless enough, because he allowed me in. I was shown into a large room, where I met Frank.

During those three hours, Frank was as personable and accommodating as I had ever dreamed. Unlike most rock 'n' roll artists, Frank did not assume a persona on stage that was different from his real self. On stage he only "turned up" his regular personality a few notches. He was…for real.

After I got home and typed up the transcript, I sent to it Wartoke for Frank's approval – and got it. Over Halloween of that year, I passed a note backstage when Frank played the Palladium, and I got invited back. Frank told me that this interview was "the best I ever gave." He said it would be included in his press kit.

Actually, the interview was never published. I never submitted it anywhere. After Frank died in 1993, I sent it to Rolling Stone. In the meantime, RS had done a cover story about Frank's death. The editor returned the transcript to me with a polite letter stating, "We already did our piece on Frank Zappa."

This, then, might just be…

The Greatest Frank Zappa Interview You Never Read In Your Life.

New York City, May 8, 1980…

Larry Rogak: Did Jane Friedman [FZ's press agent] tell you what gave me the idea to do this interview?

Frank Zappa: No.

LR: I'm a law student. I was sitting in Corporations class and we were talking about corporate responsibility and how boards of directors get away with incredible amounts of thievery because the courts will let them sweep all their dealings under the rug. My professor said, "There's some rock guitarist, I think his group is called The Mothers or something, and he said that if you want to stop crime in America, the thing to do is to put a policeman on every board of directors."

FZ: Well, that's not true. I never said that. It's not even a paraphrase of anything I ever said, so your professor is out to lunch.

LR: But what do you think of that idea?

FZ: You mean putting a policeman on the board of directors?

LR: Maybe not literally, but do you think that a lot of crime in this country is committed by people who are in the best position to cover it up? And how about the fact that if a board of directors steals millions, they may just have to pay it back but if some poor slob steals a few bucks for himself he'll wind up in jail for years?

FZ: That's right. The thing is, you can't legislate morality. If there's one thing the human race is famous for, it's being so stupid as to ignore all the danger signs of everything that's been going on through history. You can't legislate morality. You can't make people be nice. And you can't stick a policeman on the board of directors because somebody will buy the policeman. The problem is, you have people making 25 to 40 thousand dollars a year handling millions of dollars a year, and they sit there scratching their heads saying, "Why isn't it mine?" And they don't realize why it isn't theirs: they didn't earn it. But nobody wants to work for a living in America. The work ethic is a thing of the past. The unions have done away with that.

LR: When an artist makes a deal with a record company, how much bargaining power does he have?

FZ: If an artist hasn't made a record yet, the leverage is based on what the record company thinks the artist is going to sell. It's like buying pork futures. But other than that, when it comes time to negotiate, there's so many problems in having a good negotiation with a record company because the legal side of the record business is very complicated and very mysterious, and very tied up with unusual accounting procedures that vary from company to company. Unless your lawyer knows the accounting procedures or is in touch with an accountant who understands the subtleties of the way these people can rip you off, it's almost impossible to have adequate representation at the time of making out the contract and also in terms of enforcing the contract once you've signed your name on the line.

LR: You once said that frequently the same attorneys represent both the artist and the record company, and it's the record company's attorneys. Is there any way the artist can get a fair deal that way?

FZ: How can you get a fair deal? A guy wants to become an attorney. Why? Because he loves the law? No! Because he wants some fuckin' money! Do you want to sit there and go through all those dumb books for years on end because you're a nice person? You want to rake in the bucks. That's why they go. That's why your parents sent you there and that's why you're gonna get out of there. You're gonna get a good job and be real rich.

LR: Like Bobby Brown.

FZ: That's right. You're gonna go in there, you're gonna do the boring drudgery, you're gonna say "yes" a lot, stay up late, crack the books, and when you get out you get a tie, you get a suit, you get an office, and you start taking money from people who don't know what you know. And that's what the legal profession is all about.

LR: Well, it's the same as being an auto mechanic, then.

FZ: No…

LR: Well, people are paying you because they don't know how to fix a car.

FZ: Yeah, but I mean there is a slight difference: some auto mechanics actually do work. Now I'm totally an outsider to this, and I have a very biased opinion about the law, and I'll admit that I am incredibly prejudiced on this topic, but the way I see it, the attorneys who make the most money do the least work. The guy who looks the best, the tallest guy in the firm maybe, or the one who looks the most distinguished, the guy who went gray first, the guy who has the best clothes, the one who has the manicure all the time, the one who looks best with the briefcase, is the one who gets to talk. He's like the figurehead in the front of the boat. Meanwhile, you've got all these other guys, mensching [1] away in the background, slaving away, doing the research work…

LR: The second-year law students working for the summer…

FZ: Right! They're working their butts off, and this guy's getting a big paycheck, and he gets his name in the paper, and you're back there slaving away, and you know, you'll never get his job; you don't look like him. That's what it's down to. It's looking that certain way that a lawyer is supposed to look like in each different classification…

LR: Having a Roman numeral at the end of your name…

FZ: Yeah. The right tie… really nice. So how can a person expect justice from any facet of the law in a system that operates this way? You can't. You shouldn't be so naive as to expect that everything is going to come out all right. There have been exceptions, but I think that the whole process of justice is very badly managed in the United States.

LR: When was your first encounter with the law?

FZ: My first encounter with the law was when I was picked up for vagrancy when I was a teenager. I was living in a small town in California called Lancaster. Unbeknownst to me, about two years before I got to this town, there was an unspoken law in the community that rock 'n' roll was not allowed there, because a concert was held prior to my arrival that was sponsored by a lady named Elsie who ran a record store, and she brought these rhythm 'n' blues acts from Los Angeles up into the desert to work at the fairgrounds. And along with these R&B entertainers of the Negro persuasion came people who were selling pills and naughty cigarettes to the local hillbillies and so the community was all aroused that drugs were coming in because of this vile rock 'n' roll music.

LR: Were they using the term "race music" back then?

FZ: No, that was the earliest terminology, back in the early '50s, and this event happened around 1955, and they were calling it R&B then. The place was very rural. The major industry was alfalfa farming. I moved there because they started having the aerospace industry at a place not too far from there. It was a boom town. I didn't know there was an unwritten law against rhythm and blues music and they didn't want to have teenage dances unless it was being played by the high school prom band.

So I put an R&B band together and we were getting ready to put on our first dance at the women's club. With the help of some other people I had rented the women's club and we were putting on our own little dance. The day before the dance I was walking down the street and I got arrested for vagrancy at 6 o'clock in the evening and they put me in jail and kept me there overnight.

What they were doing was trying to stop the dance, but I got out and we played the dance, only to find that the entire Lettermen's Club was waiting in the parking lot to beat us up after it was over. That's when the chains started coming out of the cars of all the Negro members of the ensemble and it looked like it was going to be the "big gang fight in the parking lot."

LR: In your opinion, has the political climate in this country in the time that you've observed it really become more liberal, or do you think that for the extra rights we seem to have today we've given up something? Do you agree with one of my professors when he suggests that the Supreme Court recognizes no absolute rights but only conditional rights which must bow in the face of an overriding state interest? For example, when Japanese-Americans were placed in concentration camps [during World War II] even though none had been accused or tried for any crime?

FZ: You have to understand that the law is here only to help out the rich people. It's always been that way and I doubt it's ever going to change. Not just in this country but in everybody's country. The law is here to serve the interests of rich people.

LR: And yet, certain conservative elements say that what the Supreme Court does is tie the hands of the police and make it easy for habitual criminals to roam free.

FZ: That's only because certain types of things get in the papers and certain things don't get in the papers, and I think that may be a PR gesture on the part of certain right wing groups. It's always great to scream about law and order when it applies to street crime, but none of those people are going to scream about law and order when it comes to crime in the board room.

LR: How is it that anyone who is an independent thinker is portrayed by the media as crazy or on drugs so that no one will take him seriously?

FZ: First of all, it's not important that anybody take anybody else seriously, so that shouldn't be a worry in anybody's life. Are you trying to tell me that certain people haven't already stopped and listened to what I have to say?

LR: But not the people who should hear it.

FZ: Not true. The people who should hear it have already heard it and the only ones who will agree with me are those who already agree with me, and that's not just in my case, that's in the case of everybody else, because, since you were born free, you know deep in your heart that you're right and everybody else is wrong.

LR: I've felt that way most of my life. [laughter]

FZ: Okay. That's one of the reasons you went to law school. Hey, you know what's happening; nobody's going to change your mind. In your heart you believe you've got it wired. You're only just serving time at the law school. You know everything. Hey, get this over with, get the fuckin' paper that says I'm smart, I know I'm smart, but they're gonna give me a paper that says I'm smart, then I can go out and make the big bucks.

So the way it works is: nobody ever agrees with you unless they already agree with you. If I say something that you already know, then I'm smart. But if I say something that shows some insights into some things that are really correct in general terms, but you don't agree with it, I'll never change your mind because that's insulting to your intelligence.

LR: You changed my mind on a number of things. I'll give you an example. In 1976, Jim Ladd of KMET in Los Angeles asked your about your views on the Summer of Love in San Francisco in 1967 and the flower power movement in general. You said that the whole '60s experience was an experiment by the CIA to test the effects of LSD on a large segment of the population just as they had done to individuals in the Army. I'd never heard an assessment of the '60s like that before. Would you expand on that?

FZ: It seems perfectly logical. I have no top secret information to back that up. That's my gut reaction to the '60s: it was all fake. The concentration camps that were being refurbished were being refurbished not because of political dissention. That's no sweat. Political dissention, you shoot 'em. But you have an LSD experiment going on in a major metropolitan area, the San Francisco Bay area, what happens if it goes wrong? What are you going to do with all those people? Where do you think those camps were? Easy access to San Francisco. If those people go crazy and start murdering each other in the street, we've gotta do something with 'em. The Bay area was also used for biological warfare testing, and that was on the fuckin' news…

LR: I heard about that. They had a ship in the Bay and it had canisters of experimental germ particles which were released into the atmosphere…

FZ: Right. And one guy's father died from it and he sued the government. I saw that on the TV news in LA, and that's got to be pretty safe before it gets on TV news in LA. The demographics of the area were apparently the right kind of testing grounds for something: social experiments, chemical experiments, biological experiments; the facilities were there, it was a convenient testing place, and that's why I think you had that whole hippie syndrome happening there.

LR: What else do you think has been commonly accepted as a phenomenon when it was really well-engineered? What about Watergate? Was Watergate a different story from what we generally believe?

FZ: I don't think so.

LR: Because I've heard rumblings about how Watergate might have been a plot to get Nixon out of office because he wasn't taking orders from the powers that be.

FZ: I think that's bullshit. Let me tell you something: you are talking to a conservative guy. I am more conservative than you'll ever know. I am totally conservative. I'm for all those things that conservative say they're for, and then some. I'm interested in the capitalistic way of life, and the reason I like it better than anything else I've seen so far is because competition produces results. Every socialistic type of government where the government theoretically owns everything and everybody does their little part to help the state, produces bad art, produces social inertia, produces really unhappy people, and it's more repressive than any other kind of government.

LR: Have you read Ayn Rand?

FZ: No.

LR: Ayn Rand takes the exact same stance. She says you can only be free under capitalism. Any form of government under which the individual exists to serve the state is slavery and your life isn't worth a nickel.

FZ: Absolutely.

LR: Pick up her books; she's really great.

FZ: I don't like to read. To me it's boring. I have enough trouble getting through Time and Newsweek. Reading takes too much energy. Besides, I already know what I like. [laughter]

LR: Why is it that conservatives want a free marketplace, but they don't mind the government telling them what to smoke or read or eat or drink, and liberals want complete personal freedom but they want the government to have tight control over the marketplace and all kinds of regulations? Why doesn't anyone come out for a government that doesn't interfere in the marketplace or our personal lives? [2]

FZ: The answer is simple: bad mental health.

LR: It's as simple as that?

FZ: It's as simple as that. That's the major problem facing the world today is bad mental health. The major contributor to bad mental health is religion. Anybody who tries to run a company by a book or a country by a book...

When the Ayatollah [3] says, "My book says this and if you die here you go to heaven for this book," he's full of shit. And if Jimmy Carter sits here and tries to run this country by his book and says we're all going to be nice, he's full of shit. And you can't run a corporation by the book, you can't run a band by the book, you can't run a taxicab by the book, you have to take it as it comes.

When people put all their faith in the insulation of religion, that that is going to guarantee them a ticket to heaven, peace on earth, of whatever it is, so long as they follow these prescriptions these religions preach, it sets up blockades to progress, it sets up blockades to all kinds of creative things happening which is what I think being alive is all about.

LR: Especially if they think that no matter what shitty thing they do during the week, it'll be forgiven on Sunday when they feed the collection plate.

FZ: You bet. I'll give you a simple formula for straightening out the problems of the United States. Here it is: first, somebody told me that there was a poll taken, and people now at last believe we're in trouble. People are starting to suspect that drastic measures have to be taken to straighten our country out. And they're ready to do all kinds of horrible things to straighten the country out.

LR: Like the draft?

FZ: Yeah. Well, look. There are a few things that will straighten the country out that aren't horrible, but they won't try them. And these are the things: First, tax the church. The first thing you do is tax the church, and then you have to get them for all the taxes in arrears.

LR: How could you do that?

FZ: Hey: write it on a piece of paper and say, "This is the law."

LR: That's what's called an ex post facto law. [4]

FZ: Give them the fucking business. They have been running a con game in the United States for far too long.

LR: Large and small religions?

FZ: Large and small. Everybody pays. You tax the churches and you take the tax off of capital gains and the tax off of savings. And you'll put the budget back on the road to recovery.

You decriminalize all drugs and tax them the same way as you do alcohol. You decriminalize prostitution. You make gambling legal, and you've got plenty of tax revenue coming in for all of your social programs, and to run the army.

LR: In other words, the function of government is simply to protect us from each other?

FZ: Hey, the way I see it, the function of government ought to be: make sure you got good water to drink, somebody picking up the garbage, good roads to drive on, enough electricity to turn your light bulbs and record player on, and whatever smaller amounts of regulatory assistance is necessary to make this society work. That's what it should be doing.

The problem is that the people who are doing the jobs are more interested in perpetuating a system that guarantees them certain types of power, giving them status above their social security number, and that's their main drive. Once they get elected, they're not doing their job anymore. The day they win the vote, it's, "I'm a new man; I am now a public official, above and beyond anything that afflicts the rest of the human race." And these people are not deserving of any stature like that. They're nerds.

LR: When only one-third of the voters go out and vote, what else can you expect?

FZ: If you had two hundred percent of the voters going out, who are you voting for? Who runs? Who runs? Who's motivated to put their name on the fuckin' ugly posters on the wall? Only these psychotics.

LR: The same people who were sucking up to teachers in high school. So how could we have a better government? How can we get the people who should be up there to run the place?

FZ: First, you have to require fewer of them. There's too many jobs in government. There are too many holes to fill. And everybody who gets elected starts another committee, and it spreads like a fuckin' disease.

LR: And they hire their nephews.

FZ: It's not just hiring the nephews, though. It's setting up a committee to take care of this, to take care of that, to scrutinize this that reports to that one, and the bureaucracy builds on itself. There are just too many people contradicting each other in too many ways from local government all the way up to the Federal government. There's just too many people getting in on it.

One of the worst things, one of the shabbiest things I've seen in the last year that happened to this country is our Federal government allowing amateurs to participate in foreign policy. When a plane load of blacks goes over to have their pictures taken with Yassir Arafat, I mean, what are we doing here? [5] How can the government allow citizens to go and participate in volatile issues like that on a person to person basis?

LR: The government was just too chickenshit to say...

FZ: "Get back there!"

LR: The things that are done in the name of political expediency are frightening.

FZ: That's why it is never safe to put a religious guy into a position like that.

LR: But it makes them seem so pure.

FZ: Yeah, but you don't want a pure guy in there. You want an asshole. You want someone who wants to kick some ass in that kind of job.

LR: Why don't you send John Smothers over to talk with the guys at Warner Brothers, in a closed room for a little while? I bet they'd settle pretty quick.

FZ: I don't think so. I don't think you deal with corporations that way. That's the way they deal with other people.

LR: Well, when you learn about the structure of a corporation you find that the reason they're often so brazen is because no individual is liable for any but the most outrageous acts. The reason that a large corporation can, hypothetically, take four albums from an artist and release them without paying him is that at worst they'll have to pay back the money they made but not the interest they made on the money. [6]

FZ: Except in the case where the suit involves punitive damages and damages are awarded. Then they're exposed.

LR: That's not easy because the trend in the courts is not to interfere with the internal affairs of a corporation. Another problem is that it's hard for people to conceive of a corporation acting in a malicious manner. [7]

FZ: Especially when their logo is Bugs Bunny. So let's stop talking about it.

LR: I presume you're against the draft. [8]

FZ: Yes, and here's why: I'm against indentured servitude. I'm against people being put into jobs they don't want to do, because they don't do good work. When you're dealing with something as critical as the defense of our country, you don't want to have bimbos in there doing the job.

The volunteer army is a flop for two reasons. One, their recruitment techniques are just dumb. Totally dumb. The pitch is wrong. It's a totally mercenary pitch. There are millions of people in the country right now who would join the Army in a minute if you pitched it to them right. And they would be the best people to be in there because they want to be in there.

LR: You mean like you can sell them anything else they don't need?

FZ: No, no. The idea is, if the recruitment commercial said, "How many of you guys want to kick some ass?" That's the way to get them in there. That's what it's all about. You don't want an army of people waiting to serve four years so they can go to college. All the ads say, "Hey! Come on in! When you get out, you'll have all this money! You can go to college! Really good!" That doesn't qualify you to murder Russians or anybody else. What you need is people who really want to go and learn to wreak havoc. That's what armies are for. If you're going to have one, you want a mean motherfucking army. You don't want to have an army of people waiting to just get out, get a degree, become a lawyer, go and make some money…you don't want those people in there.

Now here's why the draft is stupid: they've got to set it up. Costs a lot of money.

LR: More jobs for the nephews.

FZ: That's right. Then, they'll have to round all these people up, they have to ship them somewhere, and they have to train them, they have to feed them, they have to clothe them, they have to pay them, and when it's all over, they have to hope they won't hurt each other. Because the kind of people that you stick into an Army under those conditions, those are the guys who shoot each other in the foot so they can get out, or shoot each other in the back because they don't like somebody. And an army like that ain't gonna scare nobody. You can have an army of 20 million men; if they don't wanna be there, the Russians are gonna laugh at them. [9]

So who's paying the tab for all this untalented material? What you want is talented material in there: people who like the military as a way of life, who have an aptitude for it and who really want to do it. That's the kind of army I'd like to see.

LR: I've always felt that, just like for any job, those who are the most qualified, those with the disposition to fight and kick ass, should be in there. A guy who gets into bar fights every weekend, shouldn't he be in the Army?

FZ: You bet he should be in the army. And especially now when there's something to be pissed off about [10], is the best time to appeal to those instincts that would make him want to join.

The other reason why the volunteer army doesn't work is because the government has allowed itself to fail in delivering benefits to the veterans who have already served. They have a bad reputation for failing to come up with the goods after the veterans went in there and did their job.

From the Vietnam thing, the claims of the veterans for things they were supposed to get that they didn't get, and no respect when they came back after serving time; and inside the military itself, bad conditions for medical treatment. [11] Not too many people came back from Vietnam feeling like they had a chance to do what they went there to do. The ones who went willingly, went for a chance to serve their country with capital letters, and came back being treated like shit while they were there, and being treated worse when they came back.

LR: I read an article by Gore Vidal in Playboy, where he says that sex is politics; that porn, prostitution and homosexuality are really political issues and not sexual issues. How do you feel?

FZ: The reason why the whole idea of smut is perpetuated is just to be used as a political tool. Without the spectre of smut, how can the knight in shining armor come in and clean up your neighborhood? It's "smut at any cost."

LR: I don't know… smut never bothered me. [laughter]

FZ: Well, you haven't been elected yet. [laughter] When you get elected, smut is going to rub you the wrong way, won't it?

LR: Why do you have such a bad reputation?

FZ: I'll tell you why I have such a bad reputation. Everything you read about me…

LR: Is bullshit.

FZ: …is bullshit, and here's why: I have been written off by the trade papers and the rock n roll consumer publications so many times, and have refused to disappear. And the audiences keep getting bigger and bigger, and somebody's embarrassed. After about two or three years in the business, everything that was written about me was negative, and was all downhill. Everyone was thinking, "It's all over." But it's not over. It's merely 15 years of getting better and doing more stuff. Once the editorial position of a publication is fixed, it's difficult for them to turn around and say, "Hey, we made a mistake for the past 12 years."

LR: So many rumors about you pass for fact. I used to believe, when I first heard it in the early '70s...oh man, I'm embarrassed to even say it...

FZ: That I ate shit on stage?

LR: Yeah.

FZ: You believed it, right?

LR: I believed it at the time because it was consistent with the terrible image you have.

FZ: They also say I stepped on baby chickens, and that Mr. Green Jeans from Captain Kangaroo was my father. None of it is true. None of it.

LR: At this point I know that.

FZ: I don't eat doo-doo. And it's so persistent, it's accepted as fact by just about everyone in the business. I answer that same question about three times a week.

LR: When Jim Ladd asked you in 1976 about your famous sitting-on-the-toilet poster, I loved your reply. Remember? You said, "That's right. I sit on the toilet. So do you. So does everybody else. But I also write and compose music for orchestras, and play the guitar and sing and perform on stage and quite a few other things."

FZ: Sounds perfectly logical to me.

LR: You come back with some of the greatest answers. I love it.

FZ: There is no substitute for common sense.

LR: The only publicity you ever seem to get is when there's a negative story, like when B'nai B'rith raised a fuss over your song "Jewish Princess." And they never even really sued you.

FZ: There was no lawsuit. It was bullshit. There was no suit with the B'nai B'rith, there was no suit with the FCC. I think that the B'nai B'rith treated me in a very malicious and underhanded manner in order to get their name in the paper at my expense.

LR: I thought it was a great song.

FZ: It is a great song. All they have to do is prove to me that a Jewish Princess doesn't exist. I don't see what's wrong, especially when a guy says he wants one. Some Jewish princess specimens are of a negative variety and anyone who takes one would be doing the world a favor. I had the nerve to say that I want a little Jewish princess; that's humorous and something that had to be done.

LR: A lot of people are only your fans because they believe the things about you that aren't true.

FZ: I'll give you an example of that. The first time I went to London I went to a club called The Speakeasy and I was wandering around and a guy comes up to me and says, "Hi, I'm so-and-so, the such-and-such player from The Flock. Remember that group from the mid-'60s, put out a couple of records on Columbia?

LR: Dimly.

FZ: Okay, "I'm from The Flock. Hey, when you ate that shit on stage I was so proud of you…" I said, "I really didn't eat that shit on stage." He went, "You didn't?!?" and walked away.

What is it with these people? Drugs have taken their toll on the American mentality. You know, the most horrible thing about drugs in the United States is, not the teenagers who are getting ripped, it's the drugs that have gone into the executive boardrooms of America. Everything that is used to modify the intelligence or the judgment of people in situations where they can control the lives of other people, that's what's bad. Because all the major financial decisions that are being made under the influence of cocaine are affecting the rest of the world. You're seeing bad decisions made by people who are hopped up bearing all this ugly fruit all over the world.

LR: How is it that drugs have become so prevalent in just the last 10 years? How did they spread from the underground to the board room in so little time?

FZ: Pretty easily. With the media to spread all of this information, it goes really fast, and that's one of the reasons why these changes don't occur as frequently or in as widespread a manner in other countries, because we have so much media here, there's so much TV to watch, and so many more hours spent watching TV here than in other countries.

LR: It's been said that the reason education is failing in this country is because the people who pull the strings in our society would rather have it that way so our schools turn out consumers instead of thinkers.

FZ: This is something that I've been saying for the last 15 years. The educational system in the United States is designed to manufacture consumers. You learn enough about your trade to do your job, to earn enough money to buy things. You're not given the criteria by which to judge the difference between good and bad; an American will never know what a good wine tastes like…

LR: Because we don't teach our kids aesthetics?

FZ: There is no aesthetic in the United States. The only American aesthetic is: number of units sold. Most is best. Biggest is best. How many shoes you sold, or how many ball bearings or nuts and bolts. It's number of units sold that makes you good.

LR: You said it first, on the cover of "Freak Out!": "Drop out of school before your mind rots from our mediocre educational system."

FZ: Hey, the library is free. You go to school, what do they tell you? "Read the book." If you want an education, the odds of meeting a great teacher who will stimulate you and teach you something are nil. The only thing they're going to do is give you a list of books to read. Why do you need to pay money? You go to the library, you go to the bookstore. You get the books and you read. If you're going to school just to get a piece of paper that says you're smart, what's that worth? Look how many dumbbells get that same piece of paper.

LR: How do you feel about the position a person is in when he fights for his rights in court?

FZ: Well, just leave a little blank in there that says, "How much money have you got?" Because that's the bottom line. The law is for the rich people. Unless someone does something to prove that's different, the whole record of the way the law has been conducted in the United States leads me to that conclusion. The law is for the benefit of the rich people.

LR: But some of the most famous Supreme Court cases have involved some poor schmuck who, through Legal Aid, went all the way up on appeal and won important rights.

FZ: There are always exceptions. But take it on the average. The bottom line is, the way it works, in general, is it's always to the advantage of the person who's got the money, to either buy a judge, buy a jury, buy this, buy that. It's buy your freedom time. [12]

LR: What happens when two giants collide in court?

FZ: It's still the biggest amount of bucks. Because then the bucks are translated into time: how long can you stand to struggle your struggle, because every minute costs you money.

LR: There's a suit that's been going on for 12 years now where the government is trying to bust up IBM...

FZ: My favorite 13-year-long suit was the guy who invented "Have Gun – Will Travel." He was a carnival performer who had the card, he had the whole "Paladin" thing, "Have Gun – Will Travel," it was his whole shot, and they stole it from him. He sued the network, the producer of the show, the writers, everybody. Took him 13 years, and he won.

LR: Who is it that controls the trends in music? Why does it seem that no musical trend takes hold unless there's a lifestyle that they can sell you to go along with it?

FZ: You're very astute. The answer lies in the interrelationship between the media and clothing manufacturers and all of the support systems for clothing manufacturers. No musical trend ever took hold unless you could dress up to it.

LR: Carnaby Street...

FZ: Disco clothes. Twist dresses with the fringe on them. You have to understand that there are forces at work here that are very scientific. They go way beyond the name of the jeans...

LR: The Hidden Persuaders?

FZ: Yeah, the real hidden persuaders, and it's in the music. In all music, especially consumer music for radio. That's the way hooks work.

LR: Do you think a person who tapes a record would have bought it anyway? [13]

FZ: If he had the money, probably. Because at least 50% of the charm of the record is the package. The person who doesn't own the package doesn't have the status of the package, to display in his own little environment as part of the decoration to his lifestyle. You are what you display on your coffee table. You have the great books of he time, maybe a few tasty little records here and there, that's who you are. Somebody comes in, they can tell what kind of a groovy guy you are as soon as they see your mess. That's what it's all about. That's why you have to get the album, because who can tell from a fuckin' ugly cassette whether you've got anything good on there? The whole idea of merchandizing books and records is not the initial way you think they would be consumed. There are peripheral types of consumption that bear of their case.

LR: Like the way that most of the people who own all the latest best-sellers...

FZ: Haven't read them. It's like people who buy pianos.

LR: And "best" is "that which appeals to the most people"?

FZ: But here's the hook: How do you know it's the best? Somebody told you it was the best. You wouldn't know it was the best until somebody told you it sold the most.

LR: It's that reinforcement I've heard you talk about.

FZ: And that reinforcement means more to your lifestyle than it does to your intellect.

LR: Why do most people need that reinforcement?

FZ: It starts in high school. In order to have friends, you have to be a certain way. Nobody wants to fuck a smart girl. Nobody wants to go with a guy with glasses. The one thing that's guaranteed to send you home to beat your meat when you're in high school is if you have a brain. Anybody with a brain is totally ostracized in American schools. So what happens? Some people say, "I can't stand it anymore! I've gotta get my rocks off! So I'm gonna act dumb." So they act dumb, and they get laid! And they say, "This is great! All I gotta do is talk dumb, drink beer, go to football games, and no problem!"

LR: And entice girls into their cars by offering 'ludes.

FZ: That's the way it really is. So as long as you have to act in a certain way, you have to bland your personality out in order to take care of your basic body functions. This leads to a whole host of other problems. Like when you get out of high school, how are you going to let the world know that you're the same as the next guy, and therefore suitable for pooching? You have to display artifacts of "bestness" and uniformity, and that's the thing: as long as the whole high school syndrome is based on "cool is best," "cute is best," "normal is best," and anybody who doesn't fit that mold is weird and undesirable and may even eat shit on stage...

LR: Or listen to Frank Zappa...

FZ: That's what happens. And one of the reasons why I have fans of any description is, I think I appeal to the people who need reinforcement for being different. There's not millions of them, but the few that are out there really like it because it helps them out. It gives them something to do with their spare time when they're not getting laid.

LR: You really go all out for your fans. No other artist tries to give their fans as good a time as you do.

FZ: I get a lot back from it, too. You think it's not fun to stand up there and be in a room with thousands of people who came there because they like you? That they're your friend? That's pretty spectacular, and I would do anything for them, except eat shit on stage.

LR: What happened to you in Cucamonga back in 1963 (actually 1965)?

FZ: Yes, that's some great story. I had a recording studio across the street from a holy roller church, with a 5-track home-made tape recorder. I bought the studio from the guy who built it, with the money I had earned from doing the score from a movie. In buying the studio I also agreed to take over his debts: his arrears in his rent and a few other utility bills and stuff like that. So I was in there recording 12 hours a day, having a wonderful time. And I met this girl who had a friend, who had a black baby, and she was a white girl...

LR: And back then --- whew.

FZ: ... and in Cucamonga, California, across the street from a holy roller church. They didn't like to stay in the studio all the time, they were living in the studio with me, and they went outside and would hang out in front of the place. We were also a black and a half away from a grammar school. And the town of Cucamonga is the intersection of Archibald Avenue and Route 66, that's all there is to it. This place is really tweezily small-town mentality, so they were out there playing with the baby, and people were just acting really weird.

The next thing I know, certain strange things started happening around the studio. A guy came in, said he was an insurance inspector for the landlord and I'm sure he wasn't, he was some kind of cop, he came in and I think he planted some kind of listening device in the studio.

The next thing that happened was, I was trying to produce this movie called "Captain Beefheart And The Grunt People," and we were holding auditions for anybody in town who wanted to be in the movie. We had this casting call for local people and we were trying out this guy for the role as the senator in the movie. One of the guys who tried out for the role was actually the vice squad guy who busted me, as I look back and recall.

So I don't know anything about any of the vice laws in this place of what the deal was. I was completely oblivious to all this stuff. Shortly thereafter, this guy comes to my place. I had this sign out front that said, "Record your Band, $13.50 per Hour." This guy walks in and says he was a used car salesman and that some of the guys he worked for were having a party on Wednesday, and could I make a movie for them, something to amuse the guys. I asked him what he had in mind and he described this porn-type event.

What he was describing, even if I wanted to do it, would have been impossible to do, especially on a used car salesman's budget. He wasn't thinking about lab costs and all that stuff. So I says, well, if you just want to make some used car salesmen laugh, how about if I make a tape recording for you. I thought that as an entertainer it was part of my civic duty to make sure that used car salesmen could have a few laughs.

So he says yea, that would be a great idea, and that he was going to give me $100, and he listed all these things that he wanted to have on the tape: certain types of fucking and sucking that were supposed to be...I mean he gave me this shopping list. Meanwhile, he's got a wrist radio on, broadcasting it to a truck outside. So I said, this is no problem, come back tomorrow noon and pick up your tape and away you go, the lads will have a fine time.

So that evening, me and one of the girls made this tape, and it had nothing to do with fucking or sucking. Nobody even had their clothes off. It was complete comedy.

LR: Well you couldn't see the bodies on tape anyway. [14]

FZ: Well, what happened was, there were so many laughs. We were squeaking the bed and doing all this stuff, and I spent the whole night cutting the laughs out of this tape, so there were nothing but grunts and stuff. Then I overdubbed some background music on the thing -- it was totally produced. And we had the final tape.

The next day he comes back, wrist radio again, truck outside, and he hands me $50 and I said, well you were going to give me $100. And the tape never changed hands. At that moment, the door swings open, fuckin' flash bulbs going off all over the place, handcuffs, they started grabbing things off the shelves, they took every tape I had in the place, they took an 8mm projector, they took any film that they saw lying around. They were just grabbing things and sticking them in boxes.

LR: Was the sheriff running for re-election that year?

FZ: Who knows? It was baffling to me. I didn't know what was going on. And they arrested me and they arrested the girl. They took us to jail in San Bernardino. And meanwhile, they are driving us to jail, and the guy with the wrist radio is in the back seat of the car and he's interviewing us and it's being broadcast to the truck again, and I found out that these tapes existed because while I was in the tank, they took the girl out and were playing them, saying [Frank uses a mock-State Trooper voice here], "This is really incriminating, and we got this and we got that and we got all these other tapes...We're breaking up this smut ring..." and all this shit. I mean, it was totally preposterous.

I didn't have any money. My father had had a heart attack and he was out of work. He had been in the aerospace industry in California and he was out of work. He was broke, and he had to scrounge around to get enough money for me to get bailed out. I got out and I went to LA and a guy from a record company there who had released one of my songs owed me some money and I picked up a couple of hundred dollars from him, and went a bailed the girl out. And we went a got a lawyer.

The lawyer told me that if the thing really went to trial, since they had taken all those tapes I had, they would play every tape I had in evidence at the trial and it would make a lot of trouble. His advice to me -- for a thousand dollars -- was to plead nolo contendre. So I said, what the fuck. even if I wanted to take it any further than that, I didn't have the money to do it. My father had to get a loan from the bank in order for me to fight the thing. I tried to get ahold of the ACLU, but they wouldn't touch it. They said the case was too small and insignificant, even though it was a matter of illegal entrapment and all the rest of that stuff.

So they take me to jail. When the thing finally goes to a hearing, they play the tape in the judge's chambers. There's a 26-year-old D.A. who is out to get me. And there's a judge, there's a vice squad guy, and there's me and this girl. And we're sitting in the judge's chambers and playing the tape and he's laughing, and going, "Hey, this is pretty good! It's a funny tape, right? What is this?"

So they plea-bargained the thing so I would get 3 years' probation and a six month suspended sentence. But the deputy DA insisted that I must spend time in jail. I had to have at least 10 days.

LR: We have to keep dangerous people like you off the streets, right?

FZ: Well, the other thing that was bearing on the case is they were getting ready to widen Archibald Avenue, and they were gonna tear down the place. So they figure they'd get me out of there...

LR: Saves the trouble of taking by eminent domain.

FZ: So anyway, on my way to the little holding tank before the bus comes to take me to the county jail, the vice squad guy comes into the place there with the district attorney, and they've still got all my tapes, everything they took out of my studio, and he says, "If you'll let the sheriff decide which of these tapes are obscene, we'll give you back everything else." And I pointed out to him that it was not in my jurisdiction to convert a sheriff into a judge. And they walked out. And that was the last I ever saw or heard of all my property that they took out of the studio. I never got it back. Including master tapes of musical performances and things that weren't dialogue, they just took the whole thing, and they never gave it back.

LR: Maybe it's still in the property clerk's office back there.

FZ: Probably not.

LR: Who is your legal representative now?

FZ: Steven Miller. He's really good. He's a real stinker, and boy is he clean. He's one of those manicured guys. He handles a lot of big cases.

LR: Frank, how many people do you think know that "Stick It Out" comes from an old piece of yours called "Geff Mijwat Vloor Bedeking Onder Deze Vette Zwefende Sofa"?

FZ: A lot. The hard-core guys all know it.

LR: I pride myself on knowing little things like that.

FZ: If you want to know a "little thing," where does "Duke Of Prunes" come from?

LR: Before "Absolutely Free"? I don't know.

FZ: Years ago I wrote a score for a Western called "Run Home, Slow," and there's a scene in which a nymphomaniac idiot girl is fucking a hunchback dwarf next to the carcass of a rotting donkey, and "Duke Of Prunes" is the music playing in the background. Later on, I added words to it for the album.

LR: Frank, it's been a real honor.

FZ: Well, I hope you had a good time.

LR: I know you don't like rock journalists, but I'm not one of them.

FZ: I know. That's why I'm talking to you.

Interview Footnotes:
1) Frank used the wrong Yiddish word here. A mensch is a stand-up guy, an honorable man. Mensching, the verb form of mensch, therefore has no meaning except perhaps the awkward one of "acting like a stand-up guy." What Frank probably meant to say was schlepping, which means to drag or haul oneself or other objects around.

2) This was before I heard of the Libertarian Party.

3) At the time this interview was conducted, Ayatollah Khomeini was the political and spiritual leader of the "Islamic Revolution" that had taken over Iran the year before, and the Iranian government was holding Americans hostage. Iran's fundamentalist Islamic government had banned all music, a fact alluded to in "Joe's Garage."

4) My point was, and I'm not sure Frank got it, was that changing the law to impose income taxes on churches is one thing. But making taxes retroactive to before the law was passed is probably unconstitutional.

5) The reference is to Jesse Jackson's trip to the Middle East in 1979 in which he engaged in a notorious embrace with Yasser Arafat.

6) The veiled reference here is to "Läther," which I was not supposed to mention.

7) In the wake of Enron and Tyco, this is one concept that has changed dramatically since this interview.

8) "I Don't Wanna Get Drafted" was released shortly before this interview.

9) For the benefit of those under 30 reading this: in 1980 the biggest military threat to the United States was considered to be Communist Russia. Times have changed.

10) The holding of American hostages by Iran.

11) Isn't it amazing how this and other comments by FZ are just as accurate today as they were 31 years ago (as of this writing)?

12) I think O.J. Simpson and Robert Blake would agree.

13) The reason for this question is that, at the time, the record companies were pushing Congress hard for a "blank tape tax" that would supposedly reimburse the music industry for the money they were losing because people were making casette tape copies of records instead of buying the records themselves.

14) A dumb and obvious comment by me, but I left it in anyway because as I said, this interview is unedited.

Available from Crossfire Publications...

CANDY ZAPPA: "...To Be Perfectly Frank..." (digital release)

Candy's first-ever album is a compilation of tracks on her own and with The Ed Palermo Big Band, Project/Object and Neonfire. Live versions of the FZ favorites "Uncle Remus," "Mom And Dad," "Let's Make The Water Turn Black," "Evelyn, A Modified Dog," "Any Way The Wind Blows," Go Cry On Somebody Else's Shoulder" and "I'm The Slime" are some of the many highlights. Candy's own compositions, "Amazed" and "Could He Be The Loving Kind," complete this exciting album. Special guests include Don Preston, Ike Willis, and Nolan Porter.

Available from Crossfire Publications...
"Chances: And How To Take Them" by Francis V. Zappa

Most Frank Zappa fans know that his father Francis wrote a book on gambling, but very few people have actually seen it! "Chances: And How To Take Them" was released by a small publisher in June 1966 and quickly disappeared after its first printing. This initial reissue of "Chances: And How To Take Them" draws upon Francis Zappa's lifelong career in teaching and working with mathematics as well as his interest in presenting how math is involved in games of chance. Francis Zappa walks the reader through the mathematical formulas of combinations and probability to illustrate the mechanics of these games of chance and why they are so hard to win. Greg Russo is a college math professor in addition to his musical activities, so he is the perfect person to faithfully reproduce all of Mr. Zappa's formulas, tables, illustrations, and analysis. This edition also contains a foreward by Francis' daughter, Patrice "Candy" Zappa!

"Cosmik Debris: The Collected History And Improvisations Of Frank Zappa" by Greg Russo

Since its debut in August 1998, "Cosmik Debris" has become the Zappa biography of choice after FZ's "The Real Frank Zappa Book." This "Return Of The Son Of Revised^2" edition (480 pages!) includes a wealth of information about Frank's early days with Paul Buff, Dave Aerni, Ray Collins and many others during the life of Pal Recording Studios in Cucamonga, California along with other archival recordings from the Zappa tape library. As always, "Cosmik Debris" is presented with Greg Russo's painstaking attention to detail and research, and as long as Frank Zappa's recordings continue to turn up, Greg will be there to give readers all the details!

"If I Could Only Be Sure: The Life Of Nolan Porter" by Patrice "Candy" Zappa

Candy met Nolan Porter in 1999 and they married in 2007. They were together until his untimely death in 2021. During the early 1970s, Nolan recorded many brilliant songs, including his Northern Soul classics "Keep On Keeping On," "If I Could Only Be Sure," and "Oh Baby." In addition to an introduction, Greg Russo contributes a section covering Nolan's early years, which leads into his time with Candy. This is the book that Nolan Porter's fans have been requesting for years.

www.ingramcontent.com/pod-product-compliance
Lightning Source LLC
Chambersburg PA
CBHW060425010526
44118CB00017B/2357